RAISING THE SOUL

ALSO IN THE 'BRINGING SPIRIT TO LIFE' SERIES:

RAISING THE SOUL

Practical Exercises for Personal Development

Warren Lee Cohen

Sophia Books

Sophia Books
Hillside House, The Square
Forest Row, East Sussex
RH18 5ES

Published by Sophia Books 2006
An imprint of Rudolf Steiner Press

A catalogue record for this book is available from the British Library

ISBN-10: 1 85584 109 6
ISBN-13: 978 185584 109 3

Cover by Andrew Morgan Design
Typeset by DP Photosetting, Aylesbury, Bucks.
Printed and bound in Great Britain by Cromwell Press Ltd,
Trowbridge, Wilts.

For my sister Donna

I hope that these ideas bring you warmth, and help you on your journey. Thank you for your inspiration and love. You have taught me much about the essence of life.

Contents

Acknowledgements

In any work there is always so much that has preceded and paved the way for it. I would like to acknowledge the efforts of my teachers and of the many contributors whose dedication and impact on my life allowed these thoughts to coalesce into their present form. Their efforts in working with me and their examples in living have made this book possible. Thank you to Eileen Bristol, Dennis Klocek, Willi Mueller, Beth Wieting and Arthur Zajonc.

I would like to express my appreciation to the many contributors who responded to my call for personal anecdotes about working with the ideas presented in this book. Your openness in speaking about these matters has been most inspiring.

Credit must also be shared with Brian, George, Patricia and Susanna whose generous insights into the first drafts of the manuscript helped me to find its final form. All the remaining faults, omissions and inadequacies are mine alone.

I would also like to thank my publisher Sevak Gulbekian and editor Matthew Barton for their encouragement.

Preface

This book is intended as a practical guidebook to help you deal with the small stuff in life: remembering the important details of your days, thinking more clearly and putting your intentions into action. At the same time it aims to strengthen you for life's more significant challenges: staying more balanced in emotionally charged situations, seeing the positive side of any—even a very difficult—situation, being more open-minded and fostering an inner mood of gratitude.

It is a pathway to help you say YES to more of what life offers you, to be open to all the abundance of life's experiences and to embrace equally the difficulties that your friends, family and complete strangers offer you on a daily basis. Each relationship you have, each moment of the day, is ripe with possibilities for learning and growing. These possibilities can also take you to the limits of your abilities, patience and energy. They can spur you on to do greater deeds than you thought you were capable of or wear you down to exhaustion, sometimes both. Experiences, especially difficult ones, can serve as a catalyst for your change and development. Others can serve as signs along the way that you are really doing your personal work and meeting life with your full potential.

Raising the Soul is organized so that each chapter introduces a different soul capacity that can be mastered in turn. Each chapter is a step along a path of encounter with challenges that commonly surface in daily life. I describe the 'hows and whys' of engaging in these exercises, which are simple to perform and may take just a few minutes a day. Practised by people in all walks of life for many years, they have proven to be powerful and lastingly effective. This book explains how you can help yourself enhance your inner being, your life in general, your interactions and relationships with others and the world through developing abilities that most likely are already living or are at least partly awakened in you.

At the end of each chapter I have included first-hand accounts of how these practices have touched individuals' lives. These stories come from men and women from North America, Europe and Asia, who work in fields such as business, teaching, scientific research and agriculture.

I have been working with these exercises with students and colleagues in many countries. At my home in Emerson College, East Sussex, England, I teach them to an internationally diverse group of students in our Foundation Year Programme. The goal of this programme is to help students (aged 18 to 80) to develop their creativity and engagement with life. Through an active exploration of history, art and the sciences we seek to deepen insight into questions such as: 'What is the nature of the human being?' 'Who am I?' and 'How can I employ this knowledge to work more meaningfully in the world?' When students return to the world and take on their work, whether it be teaching, business, art therapy or farming, they report being better equipped to deal with the demands of work, family and friends, more able to stay connected, in balance and creative. They feel a deeper sense of connection to what they have chosen to do with their lives and know why they have committed themselves to it.

I suggest that you first read through this book entirely, cover to cover. Ponder how the issues described relate to challenges you meet in your own life. Give each exercise a try as you read about how to do it. They take little time (only 5 to 30 minutes a day). They are essentially quite simple to understand, but nevertheless can be deceptively challenging to accomplish and persist with. By reading the whole book, you will gain some knowledge of this path of inner development and what obstacles and challenges you may encounter along the way.

If after reading this book this sequence of exercises seems like something that would benefit you, I wish you all success and perseverance. Begin with the first exercise. It is best to do all the exercises in the order described as their effects are cumulative and mutually enhancing, each building upon the previous ones. Focus on a new exercise each month, while continuing to do your best with the previous ones. Set the schedule as suits your life. Pick the times of day that work for you.

Real change does not happen quickly, but with steady effort deep and profound transformation will be evident. Over the years, my personal experience as well as countless conversations with colleagues and students who have practised these soul-strengthening exercises have clearly shown that doing them regularly enriches life in the most practical and lasting of ways.

Blessings on your journey!

Warren Lee Cohen
Forest Row, England
November 2005

i do not claim to know you.
rather,
let it be that i approach you
ever
with the gentle question:
yes.
yes to this moment;
to this Now
and this Us.

for yes is not just a simple answer;
not always a dead end to deeper truths.
it may also be an invitation
for the open heart
to engage this world
with wonder.

and so i approach you
thus.
that our living may be
actively sharing
an on-going moment
of discovery.

Wes Hauffe

Introduction

The Path

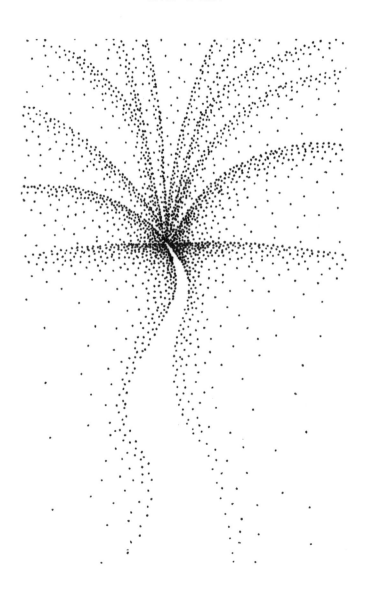

*What a piece of work is man! How noble in reason! how
infinite in faculty! in form and moving, how express and
admirable! in action how like an angel! in apprehension how
like a god! the beauty of the world! the paragon of animals!*

Shakespeare

A person can be all that Shakespeare has so beautifully
described. We all have the potential to be noble, beautiful or
even godlike. And yet we also have the capacity to be less
than these high ideals, or possibly even their darkest shadows.
It is not easy to be a human being on the earth today. There is
so much expected of us, so many choices to be made, distractions and downright hindrances. We often set up high
expectations and responsibilities for ourselves. It is not easy to
be kind, attentive, appreciative, efficient, consistent or loving, yet these are some of the most prized human qualities.
Many people wish for more natural abilities in these qualities,
but do not realize that they can in fact be cultivated and
strengthened. A certain doomed sense can creep into our
thoughts, telling us that we will always have the hindrances
and shortcomings that currently plague us. This is anything
but the case, however. You can cultivate your inner capacities in specific ways by focusing your attention and intent
on the basic, proven techniques in this book.

The exercises described here have been designed and

refined over centuries by masters in schools of learning around the world and by other great teachers, such as the Buddha, Christ and their disciples. They have proven effective over many centuries of practice in different cultures. More recently, Rudolf Steiner and others have adapted them for people today.

These seven exercises are vital and fundamental steps in developing, deepening and sensitizing your soul capacities. They are designed to help you think more clearly, feel more deeply, achieve better balance in your life, and act more decisively in meeting daily challenges. They can be done in the midst of your normal day, helping you to be more alive to all the small pleasures and inevitable challenges that life brings.

Everyone has aspirations and ideals, but many allow these to fall into a state of sleep or relinquish hope of ever achieving them. People easily succumb to habitual ways of doing and responding, often unaware of the full impact of their actions or failure to act. Henry Thoreau famously said that most people lead lives of 'quiet desperation'. Yet, a great part of this despair lies in not being able to see the way out, not being able to find and learn how to use an appropriate tool for change. Not surprisingly, these tools for change are often right there in front (or within) you, yet lie just hidden from your sight. Perhaps some crisis may bring them to your attention. But, why wait for disaster? You can also actively seek to awaken them before your life demands it. You can prepare and strengthen your many inner capacities. This will not eliminate the pitfalls that we all inevitably encounter, but will give you some tools for living through them more gracefully.

While these exercises will not instantly make your life better, they will in time and, with steady practice, help you to engage more fully with all that you really value, allowing your natural gifts to flow more easily into each day's interactions and activities. You will be able to contribute more fully to your own well-being and to that of others around you.

Each of these exercises in itself is selected to nurture a specific capacity of the soul. It is important that you follow not only the individual procedures given for each exercise but also the overall routine laid out for all seven. These exercises complement and balance one another. While learning and practising just one or several of these exercises would certainly encourage development in that specific capacity, this might lead to unbalanced and therefore potentially unhealthy development.

I therefore suggest an initial review of all the exercises. Make sure that you understand the process and aims involved in each one. Then, when you are ready to practise them, make a plan and write it in a notebook dedicated to this process. Try to do them all in the given order. Although you will probably not feel that you have completely mastered any individual exercise before it is time to add the next to your schedule, it is still best to do so. Give the main focus of your energies to this new exercise while still continuing to practise the previous one(s). In this way you can experience how they work together. It might take many cycles of practice for you to feel you are doing them well. Progress can be slow, but no one has ever said on their deathbed that they had spent too much time in contemplation. It is simply too valuable an aid for leading a rich and meaningful life to put off until some other day.

Each exercise requires little time and thus should not interfere with all your normal daily commitments. In fact, like many of my students, you may well find that these exercises help you to be more present and aware in daily life. Far from taking up time, they actually help you to structure your time more effectively. They serve to sharpen your attention and your ability to act spontaneously.

Many suggestions are given for finding times in your day to do these exercises. Strategies are provided to help you create healthy rhythms for your inner work. A suggested schedule for the entire sequence of seven exercises is provided at the end of the book. It is best to do these one step at a time and build up your practice slowly. It is far better to commit yourself to doing an exercise for three minutes a day and do it than to set goals which are too difficult to achieve. There is nothing that breeds success like success!

There are two significant obstacles that interfere with most people's practice of these exercises and their ability to stay focused in general. I call these 'the inner critic' and 'the inner chatterer'. While they will be described in more detail in the final chapter of this book, I would like to introduce you to them briefly here.

The inner critic is a voice or stream of self-critical thoughts and judgements within you. Its message can make you feel inadequate or depressed, and give you a sense of futility about anything you have done, want to or will do. In teaching both adults and children, I have seen time and again that people are their own harshest critics. All too often, the inner dialogue that people carry on within themselves is a most cruel and self-deprecating one that seeks to define how bad or wrong they are. Rather than allow the inner critic to limit your efforts and dim the inner light of your spirit, it seems preferable to try to befriend and then tame this character; for as Nelson Mandela said, 'Who are we not to allow our light to shine!'

So when you are trying to focus on one of these exercises and the inner critic speaks up with a comment such as 'You are not doing this exercise well!' 'You fell asleep again, dummy!' 'You are wasting your time and fooling yourself!' etc., the best thing to do is to acknowledge this inner voice and respond to it gently by saying something like, 'Thank you for sharing your perspective, but now I will carry on with what I was doing.' In this way, having been acknowledged, the inner critic will recede somewhat from your focused intent. Like a petulant child it will continue to visit you, but with less and less urgency each time. You will eventually be able to calm and then to master it.

'The inner chatterer' is the flow of ideas and images that naturally streams through your mind if you do nothing to focus your attention. Zen Buddhists call this the Monkey Brain, which chatters away mindless of anything else. It offers an endless stream of noise most of which is not directly related to your present choice of activity. Much of it may seem trivial upon reflection. The inner chatterer offers endless distraction that rarely serves your plans let alone your higher intentions. Remember, this voice is not you! You are the being that can choose to listen or not to this voice! This is a vital distinction.

Like the inner critic, it is best to identify the inner chatterer by name and then to tame it—without of course inviting the inner critic to harangue you for not dealing well enough with the inner chatterer. If, as you are focusing on these exercises, other thoughts or images enter into your present activity, then pause for a moment. Take a breath and acknowledge that this is the chatterer busy at work. Thank it for sharing its thoughts and then let it go. Through steady practice it will become easier to recognize these two inner voices as soon as they arrive uninvited. Recognition pure and simple will help to send them on their way, freeing up more of your attention to engage fully in any activity. Through this process you can work towards real change in how you manage your time, as well as how you speak to yourself. This taming process is described more fully at the end of Chapter 9. What is important is that you begin to see that neither of these two voices are you. They merely sound in you. You are the consciousness that is aware of them. You can choose either to listen to them or not.

This series of seven exercises is completely safe if performed as described. Their apparent simplicity does not detract from the power of their enduring effect when practised steadily. They work gently over a long period of time, and will promote lasting change.

There certainly are faster, more potent and more dangerous paths for developing the same qualities, but the negative effects are far too great to justify the risks. Austere practices, gurus and psychotropic drugs can shock you into states of inner development, but at a high personal cost. While initially tempting, these techniques can leave you in unsound mental and physical health and can threaten the basis of your individual freedom, ultimately diminishing you rather than enhancing your capacities. Slow and steady growth, on the other hand, allows for assimilation of knowledge that can gently transform itself into wisdom. The emphasis, therefore, is on developing enduring qualities and life-affirming habits of soul.

It must be added that these exercises are certainly appropriate for people already engaged in contemplative or meditative practice, as well as for those who simply want to strengthen their character. In fact the more serious you are about entering into focused contemplation or meditation, the more important these soul-balancing exercises are for assimilating the fruits of your practice, as the personal story at the end of Appendix 3 illustrates.

Exercising your soul, like learning any new skill such as playing a musical instrument or speaking a foreign language, requires consistent, daily practice. It is hard work at the start but gets both easier and more rewarding as you continue. There are times of rapid growth and development, in which you can really perceive progress. There are other times where you might feel stuck or distracted. Nevertheless, this daily practice can also be fun. It is the one gift that you can give to yourself that costs little in either time or money, and whose results are potentially limitless.

This path of inner development is work that you can and should do on your own. I hope that the suggestions given here are clear and easy enough to allow you to do this important work without the need for personal guidance from a teacher. While it is essentially individual work, many

people get support in their efforts by finding other people
who are doing or are willing to begin doing these exercises
alongside them. Then you can arrange to get together and
discuss your progress and frustrations. It can be a wonderful
experience to meet with friends or colleagues and to support
one another's personal growth.

Before embarking on the soul exercises themselves, I
would like to refer you to Chapter 10, 'What is the Soul?',
where the nature of the soul is discussed. Many people's
understanding of this word is quite vague or tinged with
religious overtones and prejudices. In this final chapter I
outline what I consider the soul to be and what I think it is
that you will be strengthening and developing through doing
these exercises. Even if you do not at present believe in the
idea that the human being has a soul or is in some way
immortal, this should in no way hinder you from receiving
the fullest benefit from this path of inner development. Belief
is not essential, but only the desire to grow as a human being.
These exercises are practical steps towards improving the here
and now and not some dreamed future. By concentrating on
your basic faculties, you can strengthen your ability to act
more clearly and purposefully in the world today.

1

Review of the Day (Exercise 1)

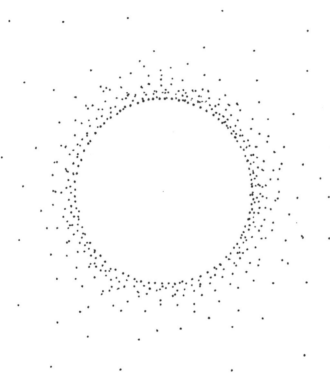

Man! Know thou thyself!

Inscribed above the entry,
Temple of Apollo at Delphi

Background to the exercise

What a full life we lead. Each day countless impressions bombard our senses. Some of these sensations we may try to ignore, like telephones ringing, billboards and junk mail. Others, like a smile from a child, a kind word from a friend or the first blossoms of spring, are treasures that make it all worthwhile. These are the lasting impressions of our lives, the true rewards of our days. Our eyes, ears, nose, tongue and skin bring us more information than we are able to consciously grasp, infinitely more, and it is our task to filter the useful from the useless, the interesting from the mundane, the nurturing from the noxious. We literally breathe in the outside world through our senses and can be deeply nourished by the simplest changes we observe. Yet much of the beauty of the world sails beyond our notice along with all the other sensations we are trying to ignore. In filtering out the millions of impressions, we can also so easily lose sight of what is truly valuable to us, all the little but precious things in life. And perhaps, these small daily events, when reviewed and linked together,

might form a more meaningful whole than we had previously imagined.

Pressures on us can be immense. We work at a job or in the
home (or likely both). We have to make many important and
also not-so-important decisions. We talk with friends, colleagues and family, shopkeepers and complete strangers.
Hopefully we have a little time for moments of pleasure or
reflection as well. However, we can be so busy at times with
what we are thinking, feeling or doing that we are oblivious to
the rest of what the world has to offer us. We miss so much,
due to all the demands that are made on us. We become dulled
and less interested in everything around us. But life does not
have to lose its lustre. We can rekindle our interest and sharpen
our senses to catch hold of all that we hold important and dear.

Within us too there is a whole world of thought and
feeling, a whole inner world that is as rich and varied, and just
as often missed, as is the external world. This tremendously
complex activity of the human soul through which we
connect with the outer world as well as with our inner
thoughts, feelings and impulses for action goes on, for the
most part, beneath our conscious awareness. It is as if we are
in effect dreaming, or as if our conscious awareness is almost
completely asleep while we live out our daily lives. This
means we overlook the meanings and interconnections of
much of what we encounter.

It is interesting to think about when it is that you are truly
most awake. For most of us, it is a precious few moments in
each day, while the rest sails by in a blur. But we do not have to
remain somnambulant. We can wake up our awareness and
begin to take steps to experience everything more consciously.

The impressions we absorb and try to digest provide us with nourishment, just as food nourishes our bodies. In recent years many people have woken up to the impact of diet on human health and the health of the planet. We have realized that our choices in what we eat can make a difference. What we put into our bodies matters. People of my parents' generation generally just ate the food that was served to them, regardless of whether it contained meat, was vegetarian, organic, had wheat, salt, nuts or dairy products, etc. in it. While they definitely preferred certain foods or for religious reasons had restrictive diets, they did not expect the variety of special diets that we now commonly have. In comparison, the kitchen at Emerson College kitchen has to prepare nine varieties of the same lunch menu each day in order to meet the specific dietary requirements of all of the staff and students. In the old days, only one or possibly two options were on offer.

Today many people take their diet, what they eat, far more seriously or at least wish they did. They sense that certain foods make them feel healthier and more comfortable in their bodies. Other people choose special foods to lose weight or to address certain nutrient imbalances in their bodies. For others buying particular foods is a political statement, a potent means of affecting social change through their purchasing power. By buying fair-trade, organic or biodynamic food, they are promoting healthy farms and agricultural practices.

It seems logical to most people that if they eat well they will feel well. If they eat too much junk food they will suffer the consequences of their excesses. There is the famous, if not shameful legal case in the USA where a lawyer created a

'Twinkie Defence' to legally justify his client's misdeeds because of the gross lack of nutrition in a diet comprised primarily of Twinkie snack cakes. Because the accused was literally starving on his diet of cakes, he was declared temporarily insane. Fortunately most of us do not need to push our limits to this extent to realize the importance of what we put into our bodies.

What food is for our bodies, sensory impressions are for our souls. Our sensory impressions nourish us to the extent that they are good for us. A beautiful piece of music can fill us with joy. A smile can change our day. Certain scents can immediately take us back to happy childhood memories. Such is the positive power of sensory impressions. But equally, impressions can poison us if we do not carefully choose what we take into ourselves and try to counteract those that are harmful. When we take in too much sensory stimulation or impressions of poor quality (for example, meaningless, degrading or violent images or information), we suffer. We have to work hard to clear our minds and cleanse our souls of certain kinds of harmful stimulation, especially from life traumas, advertising, TV, computers and movies. These are most difficult to erase or transform in our souls.

However, we do not need to be the victims of what enters our souls via our senses. We can strive to be more conscious of the soul nourishment we are giving ourselves. When we are taking in many individual images a second, we can literally get indigestion of the soul, which can manifest in sleeplessness, nightmares, poor decision-making or irritability. This can limit our ability to function well. On the other hand, the nourishment from a good conversation with a friend, a beautiful piece of music or walking through a particularly inspiring landscape can lift the spirits for days afterwards.

The task of this exercise, then, is to make the best use of all that our day has offered us, to retain what is beneficial and to counterbalance what has been damaging. You can become more alert to the treasures of your daily interactions, working life and routine activities and see in them all the richness that life has to offer. Then you can incorporate (literally, 'bring into your body') the fullness of your experiences and help yourself to learn how to more fully digest and integrate them. For this truly is a matter of digestion, of receiving all the nutrients and meaning from your life. Through this process you can realize a deeper connection between the many mundane activities that fill daily life along with all of the more trying challenges. Within these memory pictures certain events may even stand out as small miracles in which your day unfolded seemingly by plan. One event emerges as inextricably linked to others.

Looking back over your day may not only help you to digest its events more consciously, but can help you to choose better soul nourishment the following day. Thus review can also become a preparation for what is to come.

Exercise 1: Review of the Day

Looking over the events of the day, from the present moment backwards to the moment of awaking

At the end of the day (or at any chosen point in the day) find a comfortable and quiet place to sit. The posture you choose for this exercise as for all of the exercises given here is important only inasmuch as it should be comfortable enough to maintain without distracting pain or discomfort. Be comfortable, but not so comfortable that you fall asleep while trying to do the exercise. Some people choose sitting in a chair, on the floor, in bed or even standing up. Others are able to do it lying down in bed, but many people find that this leads to their falling asleep before they have completed the exercise. Find a place and a posture that suits you, your body and your home. Choose a time and place in which you are least likely to be interrupted.

To begin this and all the exercises given in this book (or rather to help you begin), it is best to take a few minutes to calm and clear your mind and to relax your muscles. There are many aids for doing this, including saying a prayer, lighting a candle, ringing a bell, taking a few deep breaths or scanning your body for tension and then relaxing it. However you choose to begin, it is important to take a few moments for preparation to mark for yourself that you are about to do something different, something out of the ordinary course of your daily life. Just as an athlete stretches before exercise or a musician tunes an instrument before playing, so too preparing for a focusing exercise will allow you to enter more deeply into the practice and possibly to find more fulfilment in it.

Now try to picture yourself going through your day backwards. Yes, *backwards* from the present moment, back to the first impressions of the day when you awoke.

Try to picture yourself as if you were witnessing yourself living the events of your day from outside, as an objective onlooker would see you, going backwards through the activities of your day—as if you are watching the video of your day in reverse, rewinding your day from where you are now back through all that the day has offered you. You are the witness of all that passed before your senses. You can also focus on all the interactions that you have had with other people that day. Try to remember with whom you have spoken, even what has been said and collect all the seemingly insignificant events that have filled your day. Capture as many of the sights, sounds, smells and tastes of the day as possible. See if you can get all the way to your first waking thoughts. Possibly even some of your dreams from the night before will come back to you. Then you have truly witnessed the panorama of your day.

Upon initial reflection some of these details may have seemed insignificant or ordinary at the time. In looking at them again, they can shine with a whole new light, for now they are placed in the context of the whole day. The details link one moment to the next. One event might never have happened had not all the other events that came before it prepared the way for it. Each moment can thus be perceived as linked to the others in a tapestry of meaning and interconnection. You could say that all that has happened is in debt to all that has come before it. Without what came earlier, what came later would be impossible. Try to remember and picture as much of the detail as you can. If you miss something or inadvertently skip over a part of your day, it is OK. Try to be patient and forgiving of your limitations. Go back to the moment you forgot and just keep on reviewing from where you left off. Just keep on going, doing your best. Keep breathing calmly.

If your mind veers off on a tangent, as is so easy to do, try to follow your thoughts back to where you left off with your review. It can be like following a trail of breadcrumbs as they disappear all too quickly. Nevertheless, try to track them thought by thought, image by image. Then continue where you left off.

Some people complete this exercise easily in 5 to 10 minutes. Others struggle to do even part of their day's review in half an hour, or fall asleep before they have completed the review. What is most important however is not that it is done perfectly, but that you have put effort into doing this exercise. It is the effort, the active exercise of soul that fosters development. This is about learning and harvesting meaning, not about being perfect, so be kind and forgiving to yourself. This is essential in any undertaking and even more important when the challenge is to develop your soul. Along this path, a genuine quality of forgiveness will serve your soul development.

If it is very difficult for you to review your whole day, then I suggest you try to review just a part of your day, say from lunch back to breakfast, or from what happened when you returned from work or school. You can choose to review a book you read, a conversation, a walk, a movie or, more challenging, a piece of music, backwards. What is most important is that you try to do this each day and better still each day at the same time. Rhythm will always strengthen your practice and will, in time, bring the best results.

After some time you may find your daily review meets

with obstacles. While the exercise often gets easier with time, it can also become even more difficult, especially at stressful times in your life. This happens even to people who are experienced in doing this exercise over many years. The most important thing to remember is to be patient, persistent and kind to yourself.

Give yourself a task in which you can succeed with a reasonable amount of effort. Too difficult a challenge might soon cause you to get discouraged and give up the whole idea, having labelled yourself lazy or a failure. On the other hand, if the challenges are too easy, and you are not exerting much effort to accomplish them, you can become bored. Then it is best to increase the level of challenge. Be more specific in what you are demanding of yourself. If you are experiencing impediments other than these, or if you would like a fuller description of how to deal with these challenges, turn to Chapter 8, 'Along the Way: Progress and Obstacles', where they are described more fully, with many suggestions for overcoming them. Impediments can be our greatest teachers. They show us exactly where we need to begin our work.

I know many friends, colleagues and students who continue to find it valuable to look back on their days for a few minutes in the evening. Many have been doing this daily review exercise consistently for years. One says that it helps her to put her day to rest. Her sleep is more sound and she has fewer problems from stress-induced dreams and insomnia. Others point to the sense of completion it gives to their days and how well it helps them to prepare for the day to come.

Another friend has a much more demanding routine. After

reviewing the events of his day, he then goes on to review the emotional stream of the day (all the ups and downs, passions, interests and angers that he felt that day). Then, if time and energy permit, he attempts to review each conversation that he had that day, word for word. While this is more strenuous than most people could comfortably expect of themselves, it does illustrate how people can take this very basic exercise and fine-tune it to meet their own particular needs.

This is an invitation to be creative, to take yourself and your development seriously. You know best what you need and how much of it you can sustain daily. Try not to worry too much about progress, just keep to it. Trust yourself and listen to the subtle advances you make whenever you stretch the capacities of your soul. Through this process you can come to know yourself better, consciously viewing how you have travelled your day. Each step into the future will be informed by all that you have made of the past.

Here is how one person describes her and her spouse's experiences with this exercise and how it helped her in a time of crisis in her life. The review of the day became a part of her healing process.

In 1997 I was involved in a traffic accident. I hit my head badly—but I was quickly back on my feet—and I was grateful for having escaped the accident with my life. Three days after the accident, however, I suddenly couldn't remember things. Then I completely lost my powers of concentration. This was a shock for me. I was diagnosed with Post-Commotional Syndrome, caused by concussion.

Although I regained my powers of concentration somewhat with the aid of anthroposophical medicine and curative eurythmy, my lack of memory was still debilitating. Post-its became my crutch. They were stuck all over the place, yet I still missed appointments and forgot many other things. My short-term memory just was not working.

What saved me was the Review of the Day exercise. Every evening before I went to bed, I did a systematic review of the day. This was a Herculean act of will, since I remembered so poorly. Soon I found that my memory was improving. This gave me hope. My life began to go back to normal. I regained my powers enough to attend a two-year course in social development and adult education. Today, I have a year left of my midwifery training, during which I have had to greatly exercise both my memory and ability to concentrate.

The review has also greatly benefited my marriage. My husband and I were going through some hectic years when our children were young. Besides renovating our house, I was also studying in school. We were so busy that we were running out of respect for each other and could feel ourselves growing apart. If nothing changed, our marriage would have collapsed. We decided to listen each night to each other's reviews of the day. This gave us a renewed understanding of each other's lives and daily tasks. Our respect for each other has grown in like measure.

Midwife
Skanderborg, Denmark

2

Clear Thinking (Exercise 2)

I thought a thought,
But the thought I thought I thought was not the thought I
thought I thought I thought.
If the thought I thought I thought, had been the thought I
thought, I thought,
I would not have been thinking so much.

Tongue twister

Background to the exercise

Children have an innate ability to give their full attention to whatever they may be doing. Like the tongue twister above, words, sounds and games completely engage their attention. Children's focus is complete and completely in the now, and childhood is often blessed with timeless spans of selfless absorption.

Adults in contrast can have great difficulty in focusing on a thought or activity with the complete, rapt attention of a child. Often we long for that kind of complete absorption, only to be frustrated by an endless litany of thoughts, doubts or a hindering sense of self-consciousness. It can be so difficult to fully give oneself just to the moment. To be taken over by the experience of the present is a much more rare and therefore cherished experience in adulthood. Usually our minds are filled instead by the endless assault of daily tasks and responsibilities, not to mention media and communication technologies that distract us from whatever we are actually doing. And rather than having control over our thoughts, they can at times (maybe most of the time) seem to wander in a rather chaotic manner all on their own. How frustrating this can be when we are trying to do something important or solve some pressing dilemma.

A friend of mine who is a doctor in New Zealand sent me an e-mail recently that clearly paints this picture of endless distraction, and even offers a diagnostic name for the condition which so many of us experience:

AAADD
Age Activated Attention Deficit Disorder

This is how AAADD manifests itself: I decide to wash my car. As I start towards the garage, I notice that there is mail on the hall table. I decide to go through the mail before I wash the car. I lay my car keys down on the table, put the junk mail in the trash can under the table, and notice that the trash can is full. So, I decide to put the bills back on the table and take out the trash first. But then I think, since I'm going to be near the mailbox when I take out the trash anyway, I may as well pay the bills first. I take my cheque book off the table, and see that there is only one cheque left. My extra cheques are in my desk in the study, so I go to my desk where I find the can of Coke that I had been drinking.

I'm going to look for my cheques, but first I need to push the Coke aside so that I don't accidentally knock it over. I notice the Coke is getting warm, and decide I should put it in the refrigerator to keep it cold. As I head towards the kitchen with the Coke, a vase of flowers on the counter catches my eye. They need to be watered. I set the Coke down on the counter, and I discover my reading glasses that I've been searching for all morning. I decide I'd better put them back on my desk, but first I'm going to water the flowers. I set the glasses back down on the counter, fill a container with water and suddenly I spot the TV remote... Someone left it on the kitchen table. I realize that tonight when we want to watch TV, we will be looking for the remote, but nobody will remember that it's on the kitchen table, so I decide to put it back in the den where it belongs, but first I'll water the flowers. As I pour water on the flowers, some of it spills on the floor. So, I set the remote back down on the table, get some towels and wipe up the spill. Then I head down the hall trying to remember what I was planning to do.

At the end of the day the car isn't washed, the bills aren't paid, the trash hasn't been taken out, there is a warm can of Coke sitting on the counter, there is still only one cheque in my cheque book, I can't find the remote, I can't find my glasses, and I don't remember what I did with the car keys. Then when I try to figure out why nothing got done today, I'm really baffled because I know I was busy all day long, and I'm really tired, but had better check my e-mail.

Unfortunately this picture can be all too true. Hopefully your days are not filled with such endless confusion. I have caught myself all too often falling into such chaos, in which the things that I want to be doing multiply, while what I actually achieve diminishes. We can multi-task ourselves into distress, accomplishing less and less with more and more effort. In addition, it is very possible that the more time-saving devices we have in our lives the more likely this problem is to arise. They seem only to exacerbate the problem rather than help solve it. Perhaps this is why so many people yearn for simpler lives, so that they have more time and energy to devote to the people and activities that really give them pleasure.

Wouldn't it be wonderful to be more in control of the flow of our thinking, to be able to follow a chain of thoughts from beginning to end without distraction, to be able to make sense of even difficult situations, to think clearly? Clear, uninterrupted thinking can help us to make better decisions and bring us in closer touch with our intuition. When our thinking can probe right into the core of the matter and intuit the best course of action in any particular situation, it becomes both warm and penetrating—heart thinking in fact. We know far more than we realize and have access to far greater wisdom than we often imagine.

Through thinking we can come to know the world and even more significantly ourselves. Clear thinking can lead to an honest and healthy self-image. Unclear or muddled thinking leads to confusion, frustration and anxiety. As the popular speaker Byron Katie notes, 'Your most intimate relationship is the one you have with your thoughts.' This relationship with your thoughts deserves some tending and will only be strengthened through challenging the assumptions you hold. It is often unclear or untrue thoughts that lead to unhappiness, anger or guilt. By thinking about the thoughts you have, that you depend upon to define yourself and others, you can come to see the source of so much misery in the world. Possibly, by seeing how untrue some of your thought patterns are, you can untangle the threads of your thinking that bind you to particular sources of pain or difficulty. Liberated, you will have energy to focus on what is true and really important in your life.

Thinking can also take you beyond yourself and fill you with ideals such as truth, beauty and goodness, justice, democracy and freedom. Through thinking you can unite with these universal ideals and archetypes, and connect with the power and significance of God or the spirit. Thinking is in fact what connects all people to what is highest in humanity, our striving and our ideals of love, compassion and brotherhood. The activity of thinking itself unites what is common amongst us. Thinking forms the very concepts on which our language and ability to communicate are founded.

While it might be tempting to try to slow the entire world down, or to wish to add an extra hour to each day, you can only really slow down the pace of your own life. Simplifying and focusing on essentials are important steps in creating more space and time. This may require significant changes in your lifestyle. Nevertheless, you can create some real change by enhancing your ability to think clearly. Even if you cannot slow down the pace of your life you can create regular moments of slowness or concentration each day. These can then become seeds, essential reminders of the qualities you would like to cultivate more in life. Soon you will notice other moments when this same seedlike quality appears and appreciate it all the more. Even if the pace of your life does not change appreciably, your experience of it will, because you will be more aware of those special moments of quietness and stillness. The review of the day as well as the following exercises can assist you in creating this inner space. They are presented here to help and encourage you to plant potent seeds that will vitalize your developing soul.

The following exercise can help to cultivate clarity of thought through a deceptively simple conscious journey in thinking. This exercise is about taking control of your process of thinking, being actively involved in seeing each new thought in connection with the previous thoughts. Keep in mind that interest is the first step towards all-embracing love. This exercise is, in essence, about learning how to cultivate interest in even the most mundane object and by maintaining your undivided attention on it to increase your ability to focus on anything. Thus it is a step in learning how to give your attention freely and completely, wherever and whenever you should choose. So while this exercise is focused solely on thinking you may well find that its impact goes far beyond just clarifying your powers of thinking, and actually enhances your ability to connect with your intuition and with love.

Exercise 2: Cultivating Clear Thinking

Focused thinking on a man-made object for 5 to 10 minutes each day

Choose a simple, man-made object, like a cup, a pencil, a pin or chopsticks. It is best for the purposes of this exercise if the object is manufactured rather than one found in nature like a flower, nut or crystal, so that you can explore the human intention that has led to the creation of this object. Choose something that has as little innate interest for you as is possible. The less interesting it first appears, the more powerful the effects of this exercise will be on the development of your ability to focus your attention.

Find a comfortable and undisturbed place to sit. Clear your mind of all daily thoughts of the ordinary kind, in which your mind flits haphazardly from this subject to that following the whims of the chatterer. Relax. Then, place before your mind this object that you have chosen to contemplate. The physical object need not even be present so long as you have a clear inner picture of how it looks and functions. First decide how much time you will spend on this (5 or 10 minutes), then train your thinking exclusively on the object in a clear and factual way. Focus on one fact about the object and then link it to the next, thus building a clear chain of thinking about this object.

First describe how this object appears, and of what materials it is made. Make your description so vivid that you can inwardly picture this particular object. Then describe how these materials were processed to make them into this final form. Think through all the stages of manufacture. Then you can go on to looking at how the object is used, who invented it and how its invention is connected with the invention of other similar ideas. Step by step follow your thinking as you deepen your understanding and interest in this simple, ordinary object. You can do this either in a stream of mental images or, if it is more natural for you, with lan-

guage that describes what you are thinking. It is essential that
your thinking be as active and under your control as is possible, that you become the director of your thinking as
opposed to the vessel in which thoughts chance to happen.
This is about learning to master your capacity to form
thoughts and to harness the potential in your thinking
process.

I recommend that you stay *with the same object* for at least a
week if not longer. A year would not be too long. Then you
can pursue similar or different trains of thinking about the
object each day and stretch your ability to find interest in this
object again and again. Some people, however, thrive with a
bit more variety and choose to switch their object even every
day. In that case it would be best at the start of the month to
make a list in your diary, choosing an object for each day of
that month. In this way your plan is laid out clearly for you to
follow through the month.

Many people find it helpful to do a little research about
their object before they begin. This deepens their interest.
For instance you can find out that the paperclip was invented
by Fred J. Kline in New York in the year 1903. He worked
for a company that helped businesses keep track of huge
stacks of their shipping records. With this background
information you can then deepen the exercise and think
about what necessitated the invention of this object, what
other ideas/industries might have been affected by it, and
how this has led to the varying types of paper clips now in
use. You may even begin to think about the essence, the
archetypal quality of the paper clip, the creative genius that
lies hidden in its very form and function

It can be helpful at the end of the exercise to review the stream of your thinking in reverse, a small version of the first exercise. This will reveal to you how consciously you have been directing your thinking. If you have been distracted at a particular point, just try to redirect your attention back onto the object. Be systematic. Make sure that one idea leads clearly to the next in a linear and logical way. The aim is to intensify mastery of your thinking activity, to be the director of your thoughts. This ability will give you a foundation for opening to gifts of inspiration that so often come at unexpected moments. You will be able to integrate the stability of linear thinking with the new insights of inspired thinking. Together they can be a powerful and creative force.

After some practice, you may notice a subtle feeling of firmness and certainty developing in your thinking. Your ability to direct your thinking is maturing. Quietly direct your attention to this feeling and notice where and how you are feeling it. Try to become aware of where it is centred in your body. Conclude this exercise by imagining that you are letting this feeling well up into your brain and then letting it pour down your spinal cord. This last step is important as it allows energy built up in the exercise to flow through the body and nurture the rest of your organism. Thus thinking enlivens your entire body and can become the conscious impulse towards generating interest and love.

This is how one person I know came to discover the usefulness of this exercise, while she was preparing for a difficult assignment.

When I was working as a trainer of female employees, I often had to travel by train and taxis to 'sell' the programme to different organizations. I was usually invited either by company personnel managers or at the request of the employees.

In the early morning, I am pretty far from my best. Sometimes the stress of preparing has reduced my sleep to desperate tossing and turning. So, on those mornings in particular, my brain was fogged and my feelings were in a knot. On the outside, I was dressed for business with my war paint on. On the inside, I was jelly. But I had read a description of the basic exercises to develop soul capacities.

In my desperation one morning on the train, not wanting to lose the client or disgrace myself professionally, I took out one of my pens and gave it a long hard look. Pretty soon I was intently working on the concentration of thinking exercise. As I got further and further along in the process, I could feel the fog lifting from my mind and my emotions come to rest. My breathing changed too. I found myself sitting up in my seat.

When I arrived at the meeting my head was clear, my listening was flawless and my emotions were in balance. After that, I took to leading participants through this particular exercise to prove to them that keeping yourself in check and working on your personal development didn't necessarily mean selling your house, divorcing your spouse and moving to Katmandu! You can start by picking up your pen and thinking about it for five minutes.

Business Consultant
Denmark

Men and women in all walks of life have found these exercises to be valuable in their life at work as well as at home.

Another colleague reveals how these first two exercises along with physical exercise are the essential elements in her daily rhythm. The routine she describes helps her to maintain her health and to maintain equilibrium despite the many pressures in her life.

I try to have control, focus and meaningful direction in my life and am increasingly aware of how the inner life of soul and the outer world merge. Inner darkness is part of this reality and there are times when fear incapacitates me. The daily challenge is to find courage and strength through rhythms, routines and human encounters to build confidence in myself to be able to embrace life to my best ability.

I work alone half of the time and rely on the computer and telephone to connect me to the wider world. My responsibilities stretch me beyond my capabilities and I struggle with feeling inept. Working on the computer for hours is alienating. The emptiness and pressure that often results leaves me feeling tense and frantic, hopeless and lost. It feels like I'm hanging by a thread over an abyss and I play with swinging on this thread or of letting go and falling. The freedom of inner movement is empowering, but the darkness is never far away.

Three main practices are part of my day and sustain me. I try to do these whether I'm travelling, teaching or working in the office. The Cultivation of Thinking exercise in the morning helps me free myself from emotional reactions to situations and find clarity in my thought. A sense of wonder results from this practice. Physical movement and time spent outside is enlivening, invigorating and balancing. Moving my thoughts and my body are restorative. The Review of the Day in the evening gives me some objectivity and helps me to find context and meaning in what happens in the day. Taking this into sleep can result in new direction. I am left with a sense of gratitude for the events of the day.

When I can build this rhythm into my daily life, I am better able to maintain equilibrium and can bring a quality of inner light into the daily challenges I face. The living link between spirit and matter when infused with light through my practices is nourishing and sustaining. From this comes the courage to carry on.

Educational Consultant
Vancouver, Canada

3

Intention in Action (Exercise 3)

Yesterday is but a dream.
Tomorrow is only a vision.
Today well lived makes every
Yesterday a dream of happiness
And every tomorrow a vision of hope.
Look well, therefore, to this day.

(From the Sanskrit)

Background to the exercise

There's an old adage that says, 'If you want something done and soon, then ask the busiest person you know.' On the surface, a busy person already has too much to do and would seem the least likely person to undertake yet another task. One might wonder how he or she could take on yet another responsibility without becoming completely overwhelmed. But someone who has so many things to do may be able to do more, having already cultivated an ability for getting things done. What is significant here is not that people can accomplish a lot of tasks, but how they do all that they set out to do. They can summon the will forces to do it.

This is the capacity we are concerned with in this chapter: the confidence to actually undertake things, to do what we would like to. How can we be more effective in fully engaging in the task at hand, and in finding time to do all those things we would like to do someday? Today is the day to begin making your dreams into realities. Not that they have to be accomplished all at once, but what better time can there be than now to begin to realize these dreams? Now is the time to nurture your ability to transform any impulse you have into action. Here we will focus not so much on doing or fulfilling any particular calling or dream, but on developing the inner capacity to translate your intentions into purposeful actions.

We all have ideas of things we would like to do one day. Some are seemingly mundane, like cleaning the house, doing our accounts, getting more exercise or writing back to a friend. Yet we can often have difficulty fitting even such things into our busy lives, let alone greater goals. There just never seems to be enough time or energy. The impulse waits until another day.

Greater life dreams can seem even more difficult to realize, almost beyond reach and thus can be quite daunting to even consider. For instance, starting a new job, creating an exercising regimen, being a better partner or parent. Either you find you take some small steps towards realizing your goal or it begins to wilt and then shrivel. At that point, rather than being an inspiration for a future action, the dream has become the burden of a dream deferred.

But how does one go about beginning to make this kind of dream a reality? Where do you start? One clear answer is that you can always begin by cultivating your ability to accomplish small tasks you set for yourself. Every small success can build the way to greater strides. A long walk must be made one step at a time. So major life changes, too, are little more than a succession of small steps in a particular direction leading towards a desired goal.

It is also possible, through these same techniques, to change your old and unwanted habits, like biting your nails, addictions to foods and media, and to alter certain patterns or common phrases in your speaking that you have decided are no longer beneficial for you to use. These take attention and a steady effort over many days, weeks or months, but can be accomplished. In fact, if you can keep at a particular habit for a month, you will probably have changed it for life. You can create new habits too, ones that serve your well-being. All of these life patterns can be transformed with a little will. And as always, it is best to start today and to work at it steadily and patiently. As the poet and scientist Johann Wolfgang von Goethe urges:

> Concerning all acts of initiative and creation, there is one elementary truth, the ignorance of which kills countless ideas and splendid plans, that the moment one definitely commits oneself, then providence moves too . . . Whatever you can do or dream you can, begin it. Boldness has genius, power and magic in it. Begin it now!

What lies then at the root of all these dreams deferred and everyday tasks that await your attention is your ability to engage your will, to find the forces necessary to inspire yourself into action

The following basic exercise can strengthen your inner ability to take hold of what you want most in life. It will strengthen your soul to be better able to take the steps necessary to transform your intentions into reality, to walk towards your dreams.

Exercise 3: Intention in Action—taking steps

Doing an inessential and unimportant task at the same time
every day

In this exercise, you set specific tasks for yourself to do every day at the same time each day. Simply by finding the forces in yourself to make this task, no matter how seemingly meaningless, a priority in your day, you strengthen your ability to set other priorities. By building accomplishment onto accomplishment, you can cultivate this very capacity to do anything that you set your mind to, creating a new kind of 'muscle' in your soul.

The task is to pick a simple activity that you will attempt to do each and every day at exactly the same time. Here as in all the other exercises, rhythm plays an important part in strengthening your capacity to bring intention into action. Daily repetition is essential, and is even more strengthening if done at the same time each day. The task that you pick is better if it serves no obvious or current purpose in your life, in other words, that you do the task in and of itself, out of a certain dedication just to doing it. In this way, you have to summon up the energy to attend to it out of an internal impulse rather than out of an external compulsion.

It is best if the task is simple and can be done anywhere. Here are some examples that have worked well: turning a ring around on your finger; shifting a handkerchief from one pocket to the other; clapping three times; moving a particular object from one place to another. Any simple activity will do, especially if it can be done wherever you happen to be.

Along with deciding on the specific task for this exercise, you also need to set a specific time for you to perform this activity each day. It is best to choose a time that is not too hectic in your day. Likewise, this exercise is more effective if you do not choose a time that is too easy for you, like mealtimes or before bed. See how close you can do this activity to the exact minute you intended. For instance, at 1:30 p.m. you plan to untie and retie your shoelaces. Do this same activity for at least a month. Each day aim to do it at the same target time. Celebrate your successes and equally try to learn from the times you have more difficulty remembering to do the activity.

If you miss your appointed time, then do the activity as soon as you remember it. It is never too late, and certainly this is a perfect opportunity to practise self-forgiveness. Try to do better the next day and to build towards success. It may take many weeks or even months of practise to be able to accomplish this activity at the set time, but keep on trying. It is the effort more than the accomplishment that will build these new soul capacities in you.

Once you get proficient at performing one challenge, add another. Work your way up to three simple tasks per day, each of which you aim to do at its own specific time. Try spreading them out through the day and thus also learning about which parts of the day are better times for you to engage your will and which pose the most challenges to following through on your intentions. It is most effective to remind yourself of the next day's challenges before going to bed the night before. In the evening, you can remind yourself (either before or after your nightly review of the day),

'Tomorrow I will do this exercise at this time and this exercise at this time...' This reminder also strengthens the will.

One colleague of mine makes this exercise into a little game. Her will exercise is to turn the ring on her finger every day at 3 p.m. If she succeeds on the first day of doing it at 3 p.m. then the next day she will turn the ring twice. The third day she will turn it around her finger three times and so on adding a revolution each day. If she forgets any day then she starts afresh the following day. In this way, she can measure how she is doing with her challenge. Of course, one must guard against pride, but playfulness can be an asset in any work. There is no need for it to be drudgery. Find a way that suits your character.

While working with this exercise, keep in mind the attitude you have towards something that really has to be done or that you really want to do. These things get done! How is it that certain appointments and commitments are relatively easy to keep, while other intentions simply slip your mind and never seem to reach fruition? Even if you struggle with being late for appointments, for example, there are always those occasions where you arrive on time. Try to notice why some commitments are relatively easy to keep while others are less so. Do certain situations fill you with anticipation, eagerness and even excitement in comparison to others that cause apprehension, nervousness or other more generally negative feelings to arise in you? The challenge in this exercise is to see if you can imbue a relatively meaningless task with the same importance you might give to meeting your child, catching an aeroplane or fulfilling an important commitment.

After practising for some time, try to notice your inner feelings when you accomplish your task at the appointed time. A subtle feeling of confidence and certainty will develop in your soul. You will begin to believe that you can accomplish whatever you set your mind to. In fact, you will feel impelled to bring your ideas into action.

One friend, looking back on her experiences with this exercise, wanted to share the following story. Much to her surprise the effects of having done this work had an impact on her that lasted long after she had finished doing the exercises. She noticed she had new abilities to deal with difficult challenges that she had never before faced.

In reflecting upon my work with these exercises, especially the strengthening of the will exercise, I have made a surprising discovery. The times that I have been most successful in doing them regularly have come just before two crises disrupted and then rearranged my life: a divorce and later a career change. Before these turning points, I was able to enter fully into the challenge of doing the exercises without being distracted by the demands of my daily life. With a real sense of accomplishment, I was able to pursue and have some success with these exercises. These were deeply satisfying moments. I do not now blame the exercises for the chaos that then happened in my life, for they did not precipitate these changes. But I can see now that having done the exercises for many years gave me a certain strength and resilience to face up to the realities of the situations I was later to face. I was better able to deal with the uncertain demands my life was placing upon me.

Through being able to do the will exercise in particular, simple tasks every day at the same time, ones for which there was no outward command, I felt inwardly grounded and self-controlled. I was able to take hold of my will, nurture it and have clearer thinking as well. Despite the pressures I was under from divorce and later changing careers that kept me from continuing with these exercises for a while, I felt an inner strength that carried me through these times of trial and that still lives in me today.

Teacher
Olympia, Washington, USA

4

Balance in Feeling (Exercise 4)

He who binds to himself a joy does the winged life destroy. But
he who kisses the joy as it flies lives in eternity's sunrise.

William Blake

Background to the exercise

Feelings are fleeting tastes of our inner, soul world that
continually transforms in response to both inner and outer
stimuli. Our feelings give us a supple window into this more
hidden and completely individual dimension of our being.
They inform us about how we are doing at any particular
moment and, as a result, can change in an instant. Feelings
serve as signposts. If a personal need or value is not being met,
then a feeling of dissatisfaction, frustration or anger might
arise. On the other hand, if our needs or hopes are being met,
then we may well experience a deep feeling of satisfaction or
joy. Unfortunately, most of us are relatively unaware of what
we are feeling at any particular moment. Our society, for the
most part, has educated us to be this way, to tame, ignore or
suppress our feelings. This may be especially true for men.
Without being connected to our life of feelings, we risk
missing out on much of the joy and vital information that our
inner life can offer us.

In adolescence, the whole inner world of feelings first
opens before us like a flower in blossom. It emerges in full
colour and complexity, with a new inner power and vitality.

With tremendous surges of emotion, adolescents begin to feel the heights of passion and the depths of woe, the joy of belonging and the pain of feeling outcast. Their whole world, spurred by the advent of puberty and the complexities of sexual maturity, can lead them mercilessly from the heights of joy to the depths of sorrow and back again. Similarly, although usually with less raw intensity, our feelings as adults can be powerful enough that they either impel us headlong into activity or inhibit us from doing much of anything. We can become inflamed with our wants, desires and passions and do things that we never would have done before. We can yell at a colleague out of frustration, or do something that we later regret having done. It can be all too easy at times to get carried away in our impulses. At the opposite extreme, we can become frozen in doubt, self-loathing or depression. We can become paralysed by the seeming meaninglessness of it all. Either of these extremes can leave us feeling at the mercy of our feeling life. We can become its slave until we learn how to harness and balance its tremendous strength and potential. In extreme cases of imbalance, our souls can plunge into mental illness, depression, anxiety, bi-polar disorders or other extreme, possibly even suicidal states.

But our emotions do not have to reach these extreme states of imbalance to keep us from living fully. Even a subtle sense of sadness, feelings of hurt or anger, or hopelessness at being unable to achieve some goal can keep us from fulfilling our potential. A cloud can descend on us, which comes to seem our very nature and blocks our vision of its silver lining—of the sun shining everywhere else. It is a matter of perspective and gaining control over the perspectives that we choose for seeing ourselves, others and the world.

Likewise—although perhaps harder to notice—is the fact that excessive expression of laughter or joy can keep us from feeling the full depths and complexities of our inner soul life as well. In expressing our happiness or, perhaps, in feeling that we are only safe to express positive emotions, we wall off the rest of the spectrum of feelings that we all naturally have. The darker or more negative emotions are still there, but remain unacknowledged and simmering. Trying to be entirely happy and positive all the time is as unbalanced as wallowing in a dark cloud. We can stretch ourselves beyond habitual ways of feeling, and broaden our entire feeling life by travelling a middle way.

Part of the challenge in 'growing up' is therefore to learn how to harness the power and sensitivity of our emotional states for our own benefit, rather than letting them control our moods, thinking and actions. Being in tune with our feelings can help us to live more fully in ourselves and to have more to contribute to the well-being of our friends and loved ones. In a certain sense, our awareness of feeling is like a weather report on our inner weather. It can tell us just how we are doing at any particular moment and alert us to changes within as well as changes outside ourselves. But many of us have difficulty in knowing or being able to read just what this inner weather is trying to tell us about the relationship between our environment and ourselves. Marshall Rosenberg, the founder of Nonviolent Communication, has described our struggle with emotional awareness in the following words: 'Our emotions can have the tonal complexity of a full orchestra, but for many of us they sound more like a band of kazoos.'

In this exercise we can begin to discover and to explore what enables us to experience the broadest possible range of colours and tones in our feeling life. In this way, we can come to know ourselves and to appreciate with more detail and clarity our interactions with the world. Our interest and capacity to be interested in and love others will increase with the knowledge and strength that can come from seeking balance in our feeling life. It will give us more room to be patient and understanding and, equally, to express ourselves clearly.

Every day most people experience a whole variety of feelings, both so-called positive and negative feelings. Although you may only be conscious of a very small percentage of them, more careful observation will reveal a number of others besides the ones that you are in the habit of noticing and supporting. These others either escape your notice or possibly you actively work at suppressing them. The object of this exercise is to create more space for and an increased awareness of your inner world of feelings. This will allow you to be more conscious of these feelings and to work more consciously to bring them into a healthy balance with one another. It will also help to control habitual ways that you express (or suppress) your feelings and therefore the effects they have on you and on your relationships.

★

Unlike the first three exercises, the next four need to be practised during the course of the day and then reflected upon in the evening (similar to or along with your Review of the Day). You can choose to focus on them throughout the course of the entire day. Or if this seems like too strenuous a challenge, then you can pick a more limited part of the day in which to practise them. For instance, you could choose to do this exercise during your lunch break, while commuting to work, during difficult meetings or at home after supper. The choice of when in the day to attempt this and the next three exercises is best left to each individual. Plan on doing this exercise when you can give it the most concentrated attention without detriment to your regular daily responsibilities.

With this and all the subsequent exercises, give primary attention to the newest exercise that you are attempting, but still continue to practise the previous ones. They will prepare the way as well as help to harmonize later exercises. Also continue to write down your intentions and your experiences in a notebook. Keep track not only of your progress, but of your efforts, for it is the effort you make, rather than the accomplishments you achieve, that is most strengthening for your soul.

Exercise 4: Balance in Feeling

Consciously living with your feelings before expressing them

To begin with, it will be helpful to write down any habitual modes of feeling that you have. List your most commonly experienced feelings. Then, write down the feelings that you would like to experience but rarely do. This will give you a starting picture and help you to guide and chart your progress throughout the month. Refer to this list regularly and alter it as your experiences dictate.

Always, as in any exercise, you have to start from where you are, value who you are in the here and now and work without self-criticism. It is of little use to wish you were a more positive person and then accuse and criticize yourself for every less-than-positive thought you now have. Empathy for yourself is an essential starting point on this path of self-knowledge.

The focus of this exercise is simply to control how you express your emotions when you are experiencing particular feelings. It is not to control what you are feeling, but just to delay your expression of it so that you can come closer to knowing the pure feeling itself. The challenge is to stay conscious of your feelings a bit longer than you would usually do before you give expression to them. You are in no way trying to suppress any emotion, only your automatic (and often unconscious) response to it. This will heighten your awareness of your habitual modes of feeling and their typical responses.

If you are someone who is quick to cry in certain situations, challenge yourself not to cry in such a situation or to wait a bit before you cry so that you can come to know this feeling that impels crying. You can develop a fuller relationship with the complex impulse that has led you to the frequent activity of crying. Keep in mind that there is nothing whatsoever wrong with crying. It can be a wonderful release of tension, and many people (especially men like myself) certainly wish that we had greater access to it. But in this exercise, you can cultivate, through compassion for your inner world of feelings, a deeper relationship with the source of this emotion. Neither crying nor laughing is *the actual emotion* a person is experiencing, but merely the outer expressions of a mysterious inner process. This exercise allows you to get in touch with the deeper sources of your world of feeling. Then you may feel the world far more profoundly and find greater freedom in when and why you choose to express emotions. The tears will be all the truer for having been dwelled upon.

At the opposite end of the spectrum, some people are prone to smile or laugh at appropriate and/or inappropriate times. Laughter can be inspired by joy, but also by nervousness or discomfort. You can challenge yourself to feel the impulse to laugh and wait before you give it expression. Far from suppressing your inner joy, this will allow you to feel it all the more deeply, to live with it a while before giving it away. The act of laughing itself can actually dissipate the inner feeling that has led to it. Live with this feeling for a few seconds and enjoy it all the more. Your laughter will then resound with a deeper sense of joy.

We all know people who come to anger too quickly and perhaps express it too freely. The exercise can help you focus on this. But perhaps, on the other hand, you are a person who feels fairly balanced but has a difficult time giving expression to certain feelings. For you the exercise offers the opposite challenge. Look for an opportunity to express a feeling that you have had difficulty in expressing, give voice to a frustration you are feeling, to ask for help when needed or to show vulnerability or sensitivity to others. The objective is to find a balance between your inner feeling and your outer expression of those feelings. These need to be in a healthy dynamic balance so that you can both know yourself and connect vitally with other people. It is as unbalanced to express too little as it is to express too much. Each of us can become more aware of how we stand in this balance.

Some may worry that this exercise could detract from their spontaneity in living and being in the moment. Certainly this exercise will limit the spontaneous expression of some feelings while you are engaged with it, but it will only deepen your inner experience of these same feelings and should not interfere with your usual responsibilities or relationships. So it is not a question of never expressing your feelings, nor of always expressing them, but of trying to know them better before you express them, for the duration of this exercise. This delay could be as little as a second, if that is what allows you to develop more consciousness and a deeper understanding of them. It is rarely possible to know for someone else which exercises might open the most profound doors. Work patiently and keep to your planned rhythm. Steady practice over a month will shed much light on this obscure inner realm and give you more skills in how you choose to express it.

Here is a personal anecdote that I would like to share about my less-than-balanced work with this exercise. The process was important for my journey, though certainly not something that I could recommend for others. You be the judge. Here is my misadventure in the pursuit of equanimity.

I was interested in understanding my feeling life better as I had always perceived myself as being fairly calm and even-keeled. So I decided that for a year I would concentrate on the Balance in Feeling exercise and that I would meditate on the word 'Equanimity' every morning. I must add that I was not at that time practising the other six exercises in due proportion.

As I first began learning more about my feeling life, everything seemed to be OK. But then the emotional highs and lows, as if to test me, rocked my life in a most dramatic fashion. In a surge of romantic ecstasy I proposed to my girlfriend that we get married. She accepted and we had a lovely wedding with a joyous celebration. It was great! But then ... then, in that same year, we came to realize that the marriage was not working for us. There ensued a rapid divorce and a painful, emotional separation process. My feelings crashed from their highest peaks down to their lowest troughs. I felt pummelled by the surges of the most varied and powerful emotions that I had ever felt, truly a low of lows. Yet, I kept afloat in it all. Then amidst this turmoil and wreckage, perhaps even because of it, I was able to discover the next steps I wanted to take in my life. I stepped from educating children in a Waldorf (Steiner) School to finding my way to work creatively in adult education. Without the chaos, I am not sure if I would have seen these next steps so clearly.

In hindsight it was a very important and life-affirming year. I truly felt my feelings in a way that I had never before experienced them. I cannot in all honesty blame the Balance in Feeling exercise for the apparent chaos in my life, or even claim that it caused these events to transpire. It might have all happened anyway. Nevertheless, I do feel that in some way this practice magnified both the intensity of the emotions I was feeling as well as my ability to deal with them creatively and constructively. It helped me to see more clearly what I most valued in my life. And it has also taught me in the most concrete way the importance of balance. Now when I set out to do this exercise, and, I must add, still with some trepidation, I try to work with just one emotion at a time. Presently, my practice of this exercise is much gentler without any of the upheaval that I described above. But I still experience some hesitation in this realm of feelings, as I know just how much I have yet to learn.

Warren Lee Cohen
Forest Row, England

5

Positive World View (Exercise 5)

Whatever befalls the earth befalls the sons of the earth. Man did not weave the web of life; he is merely a strand in it. Whatever he does to the web he does to himself.

Chief Seattle

Background to the exercise

There is a wonderful apocryphal legend in which Jesus and two of his disciples are walking together and see the rotting corpse of a dog at the side of the road. The disciples cringe in revulsion at the sight and smell of the rotting flesh, repulsed by the ugliness of death and decay, the physical end we all must face. Covering their noses, they quickly cross to the other side of the road. Jesus, in contrast, draws closer to the dog to look more carefully, then simply beckons his disciples to notice the dog's beautiful white teeth. Amidst the stench and the work of maggots, he is able to perceive the beauty of the dog's strong, well-formed teeth. Even in this most challenging example, the rotting carcass of the dog, he could see pure beauty.

Positive people have a way of finding what is best in any situation. No matter how difficult or painful it might be, they have a unique skill of finding joy, connection, meaning or even important lessons in everyday events. Their positivity is contagious and a guiding light for those who are fortunate to know them.

It can be so easy, however, when watching the television or reading the newspaper, to become saddened, angry or apathetic at the general state of violence and division in the world. Wars, starvation, natural and man-made disasters, crime: this is not a pretty or an easy picture to live with, yet this is our world, or at least it is one view of our world, which the media portray. But it is not the only perspective on world events. There are a great many other notable contributions that people are making for the betterment of others, life on this planet and the environment. While it takes a bit of searching to find this good news, there are other perspectives on which to focus our attention, such as noting the achievements of individuals, appreciating the beauty in nature, and celebrating the contributions that someone has made towards another's well-being.

The perspective by which we choose to view an event affects us in the most profound ways. If a person can learn to find the positive, the hidden gem in even the most difficult experience, then just about anything is possible. Change and healing can begin their work to bring human souls back into connection with all that shines to them from this world and beyond. Any event can then become an opportunity for learning, growth, or just for appreciating the beauty in another being.

By learning to find the 'good' in a variety of small ways in our daily and working lives, we can build a capacity within ourselves to recognize this quality in more and more aspects of our lives. By taking responsibility for how we choose to see and judge events, we can begin to make a more constructive impact on our families, friends and colleagues.

As a teacher, I have found in many situations that to see the best qualities in a student, no matter how challenging his or her behaviour might be, has allowed me to find a way to help the student through those same difficulties. Seeing the positive aspects, the life-serving needs that motivate the student's actions, has also given me more compassion to bear with a student's struggles. This same quality of trying to see the best in others can be very powerful in just about any kind of relationship. It truly helps the best in them to emerge. So often our expectations (for better or worse) are met. So why not try focusing your attention on a person's best attributes and see what happens. It may surprise you how well things can work out.

It might be objected that this is really seeing the world through 'rose-tinted glasses', making even the most heinous acts appear palatable. This is definitely not what is intended. Seeing only the rosy aspects of things would be as unbalanced as seeing only what is wrong with the world. The objective is rather to create for oneself the possibility of seeing an experience from many, mutually balancing and therefore life-affirming perspectives. Most of us have had ample training in critical thinking. Now we need to learn how this can be tempered and balanced with a more positive world view that enables us to work creatively and lovingly in the world.

This is the path of compassion, empathy and healing, and of seeing the light despite the apparent shadows or darkness. This is the path that wise people have always been able to discern and navigate no matter how great the challenges. They are able to find the love and light in even the greatest of earthly calamities. There are many examples of people who have survived the horrors of brutality, discrimination and war only by recognizing the light that shone in the heart of their oppressor. In acknowledging this human striving for love and acceptance that is common to all people, these few were able to transcend the horrors of their situations, maintain their own mental and physical health and be available to help others. Positivity became a constructive force in their souls.

Here is one remarkable example relayed by an American doctor, George Ritchie, in his book *Return from Tomorrow* (see page 147). At the end of the Second World War, Dr Ritchie came to Germany to attend to the wounded soldiers and people who had been imprisoned there in the labour and death camps. In particular he described meeting with one most unusual prisoner who made a profound impact on him.

Wild Bill Cody was the name the liberators gave to a Polish inmate at the Wuppertal prison camp in Germany. When the Americans came to liberate the prisoners at the end of the war, they were struck by the health and vitality of this one man, whom they assumed had only been in the camp a short while. As it turned out he had been in the camp for nearly six years, since 1939, living on starvation rations and in a most oppressive atmosphere. He was surrounded by degradation, humiliation and death. Scarcely a darker time could be imagined. Then the liberators learned that he had been imprisoned in the camp immediately after he had witnessed Nazi soldiers murder his wife and children as well as many members of his community. He had seen them lined up and shot. He had plenty of reasons to hate, to be bitter and to want to seek revenge. However, he described to them that at the moment of his greatest despair, at losing all he had held most dear, he knew that he must forgive his captors (and the murderers of his family). He must forgive them completely and learn to see the divine spark that also lives in the hearts of these Nazi soldiers. And so he lived for six years in the prison camp and soon became the respected mediator between different ethnic groups that had little more affinity for one another than they did for the Germans. He spoke many languages, but most importantly he spoke the language of humanity, of forgiveness and positivity. This unusual quality not only saved his life, but also was a source of tremendous strength for all who have described meeting him. He was a source of hope for all who knew him and was equally respected by prisoners of all nationalities. One could say that Wild Bill Cody's incredible inner qualities of love and forgiveness allowed him to ascend to the highest levels of humanity while facing its darkest challenges.

There are countless other, though usually less extreme, examples of people rising to meet challenges that show how the clear light of positivity can shine on and enrich the lives of others. These are the people that give us hope and can show us out of the ways of our misfortunes. The hardships do not disappear. It is the way that we perceive them that changes. Often just a little change in perspective can be enough to help us pull ourselves out of the darkest difficulties and lead much more meaning-filled and fulfilling lives.

For some people, acknowledging and loving a great teacher or saviour can be a giant step in the direction of cultivating positivity. It offers an example by which to guide one's life. This can be significant, but it is not the only way.

You can start with being more mindful of the efforts others around you are making. Notice all that is worthy of praise. Celebrate the little miracles that happen each and every day. Then you can take the next step by striving to find positive qualities in people or situations that at first are not so easy for you. Even in a situation where you have felt wronged, you can challenge yourself to find something that was good or helpful in the situation. Maybe there was a lesson learned that could only be learned through this sort of difficult experience. It is possible that you would not have learned it through any more gentle means.

You can celebrate the determination of a blade of grass that grows against all odds through a tiny crack in the sidewalk. You can understand that a baby's crying is its first efforts at learning to communicate. Possibly you can find some value in the difficulties that come your way each day or in the conflicts and violence flaring up in the world, because they may lead to the development of some new qualities in humanity. Perhaps our environment is threatened so that we can awaken to our responsibility for taking care of this planet. All of life presents opportunities for learning, developing and for helping others if we can only recognize them as opportunities.

Exercise 5: Positive World View

Looking for the positive in the events of each day

This exercise is best if carried in heart and mind throughout the day and then reviewed at the end of the day along with the daily review. (Do not let go of this most valuable 'Review of the Day' while attending to the other exercises.) If this feels like more than you can commit yourself to, choose one or more limited time periods of the day such as your lunch break, your journey to work or the first hour of your day. Again, regularity and rhythm will help you with your efforts towards cultivating a positive, life-affirming perspective.

The challenge is to seek out all that is good, praiseworthy, helpful or beautiful in any and every situation in your day. Look for it in all experiences, both the pleasant and the unpleasant, the mundane and the special. Look for it in all realms of human endeavour as well as in all the kingdoms of nature. Challenge yourself to find it in any situation, whether it is your own or that of others, whether things are going smoothly or if someone is experiencing difficulty. Try to find some silver lining in even the worst circumstances. It can often be easier to appreciate the workings of positivity when you have the distance of observing the interactions of other people. Your feelings are not as easily triggered as they would be in a more personal situation. This allows for more objectivity in your perception of the situation and it would be a good strategy to begin doing this exercise. Each day encourage yourself to notice more of the positive, the good, the beautiful and the praiseworthy. Push yourself to look for it in ever more challenging places. You are in effect developing a new organ of perception, a new way to process the experiences of your senses. Progress does not always come quickly. Nevertheless, with steady practice you will notice that you begin to see events in a new light. Even amidst tragedy there will appear some hope for the future.

The exercise of positivity itself creates the possibility for experiencing ever more positivity. And yet it does not in any way eliminate the possibility of seeing the world in other (more judgemental) ways. You should not hope through performing this exercise to eliminate frustration, evil, ugliness or untruth. What will begin to change is how you perceive and respond to them. When confronted by a disturbing situation, you can begin to discern how something has come to be the way it is rather than simply criticizing it outright. Every situation has had to develop into its present state. You can begin to appreciate all that has gone on before to create the present circumstances as well as what good might emerge from the current tensions. Even amidst apparent evil, you can search for what is good or valuable. When confronted by things that appear untrue, you can look for truths that lie obscured. By always looking deeper into what the world presents to your senses, you can begin to see whole new layers of meaning and connectedness. You might begin to trust that everything has value and purpose even if it is not immediately evident. Your inner attitude can have a profound effect not only on how you see the world, but in how you choose to act in it. Acting out of an inner impulse of positivity can become a real force for positive change.

A friend of mine, who farms vegetables for a living, shared with me this story about how she could see the effects of her inner attitude on the growth of the plants she was trying to raise. In this case, the plants were her strict teachers. They revealed to her the impact of her emotions.

As a part of my spring rhythm, I was planting seeds in the greenhouse many days a week. The work was repetitive and allowed much time for contemplation. I always had a hunch that my state of mind while performing a task might influence the outcome, but what I observed that spring shook me with its display and made my intuition that much stronger.

One planting day I was particularly upset and angry. I went on however planting as usual. I poked seeds into the soil, watered them and placed the trays of seeds with all the others in the greenhouse. Two weeks later I saw the strangest, most deformed looking plants in these trays. They looked so twisted and unhealthy that I decided not to transplant them into the garden with the others, but to add them to the compost.

There in the malformed shapes of their leaves and stems appeared the image and possible effects of my anger. It was not a pretty sight. While I hesitate to say that my anger 'caused' those shapes, it certainly did appear as if my working mood imprinted itself on the growth of those seeds. Those plants bore the imprint of my inner attitude, which had been anything but healthy that day.

I had felt strong anger only that one day while I was sowing the seeds, and only that day's plants looked deformed. The others, planted in exactly the same conditions except for my mood, were fine. I have since come to notice the impact of my emotions on the life at the farm on many different occasions, not only with the plants I grow, but with the food I prepare and in meetings with people. My attitude clearly impacts on many of these situations. This can be equally strong in the other direction as well. A particularly harmonious working mood seems to support not only healthy plant and animal growth but healthy farmers as well.

Farmer
Eugene, USA

6

Open Mind (Exercise 6)

To see the World in a grain of sand
And heaven in a wild flower.
Hold infinity in the palm of your hand,
And eternity in an hour.

William Blake

Background to the exercise

Truly creative people, or people in truly creative moments, are able to find new relationships, completely new ways of seeing how things are interrelated. Other people may have looked at or studied these same situations yet they were unable to recognize what the creative person saw in that one instant. Discoveries and intuitions often happen in a flash of creative inspiration. While they are long planned for and sought with endless hours of toil, the new idea or discovery appears by itself and usually quite unexpectedly. All of a sudden a whole new way of understanding emerges, only because the person found another way in which to view the situation at hand. A new creative impulse or paradigm emerges which then leads others to also see and explore the situation from this new perspective. This process is true for great artistic and scientific discoveries as well as the seemingly mundane decisions in our daily lives. It is only our previously held ideas, convictions and points of view that keep us from seeing the myriad of other possibilities for solving problems and for growing in turn. Learning seems to happen in a rhythm of spurts and rests. Having an open mind allows those leaps of awareness to spring into your consciousness and broaden your perspective.

William Blake, for instance, dedicated his energies to cultivating an ever-fresh and alive mind so that he could reach beyond his current limitations and search more fully for the deeper truths of human nature. His pathway was through the arts. He strove continually to be more open-minded, to see things from fresh, illuminating perspectives.

Likewise, the renowned scientist Isaac Newton sought to uncover the mysteries of the world. Like countless people before him, he observed how apples fell from trees: always towards the earth and never the other way. No one before him concluded that there existed such a law as the force of gravity. This concept, this dynamic relationship between apples and the earth was his sudden realization. He then went on to describe this invisible force in terms of mathematical formulae that applied not only to apples but to people, buildings and the movements of the heavens. Never before had anyone seen gravity, let alone described its mechanics in detail. How, then, was he able to make this leap of first perceiving and then knowing something so revolutionary? Furthermore, how was he able to develop the language with which to accurately describe this entirely new concept to other people? Gravity had never been thought of before let alone described. Newton discovered not only the new idea but also created new language and concepts to describe how it worked.

An important question to explore is what might prepare us to understand something in a new way or, the opposite, what might keep us from comprehending something directly in our field of vision. Whenever we look at something we almost instinctively try to determine what it is, whether it's safe, whether it's useful. However, once we have determined what something is and whether it is desirable or not, then we cease to look at it in the same way. The quality of our discerning grows much less acute. In a certain sense we become less interested in what we actually see and more in thinking about the type of thing that it is. We no longer see 'the' apple tree but 'an' apple tree. We stop noticing what makes it individual and see what makes it part of a group or a concept. The work of our senses takes a back seat to the working of our thinking. In general, we think about the object rather than continue perceiving new qualities in it. We classify it, put it out of our mind, so to speak, and then move on to process other information.

Similarly, we may have certain biases and/or prejudices that keep us from seeing a person as an individual, focusing instead on the race, religion, sexual orientation, social status or professional group people belong to, and easily forgetting to see what makes them unique. Perception of the individual is squashed beneath the weight of stereotypes. Or something about someone may tell you that this is not the type of person you are interested in getting to know. Then, no matter how wise or wonderful he or she may be, it is unlikely that you will be open to having a real conversation. Your initial judgements keep the reality of the person hidden from you.

Just as judgements protect us from unwanted interactions,

they also limit our field of experiences. Of course, we all have to make judgements about what we give our attention to. This filtering of the mass of daily stimuli is essential to our health and well-being. As we saw in Chapter 1, our modern world offers endless information, distractions and advertisements. We would become sick if we absorbed it all. Nevertheless, it is also significant that in making certain judgements, in filtering out large volumes of information or in holding certain prejudices, we limit ourselves from getting to know these other aspects of the world. We both protect ourselves and yet keep ourselves from understanding what is there before us.

In our desire to be safe or in wanting to feel secure, we draw boundaries around ourselves that prevent us from meeting and coming to know new qualities in other people and in the world. These boundaries can be extended in a careful and controlled way to create the possibility for life-enhancing discoveries.

Exercise 6: Open Mind

Stepping beyond previously held beliefs

In order to create an open-minded mood it is helpful to come to know what boundaries, judgements and prejudices you currently have that filter the way you understand the world. Make a list of the most deeply held prejudices that you have (e.g. I do not trust this type of person, this group of people is better than that other group, or people who dress like that are . . .). Get these thoughts out in the open at least for yourself. Name them so that you can begin to look at them with a bit more objectivity. Many of these you have learned at a very young age and may be difficult to identify. They can be absurd or ugly and can often be hurtful. Look at them and try to become more aware of these judgements that are deeply part of you, though also deeply unconscious. Take a few days—maybe three—to steadily add to this list and to check it for accuracy. Review the list and add in subtler details to build as clear a picture as possible of what limits your ability to have an open mind, free of prejudice, judgement or bias. It might not be possible or even desirable to confront all of these biases; nevertheless, to know that they exist is a huge step in cultivating soul capacities.

Once you have established this base line of your currently held judgements, then you can proceed daily to try to stretch yourself a bit further than the day before. The objective is to create flexibility and openness in your ability to take in new experiences. Like the Positive World View exercise, this exercise is best done throughout the whole day or, if that seems too much, in some specified period of the day (e.g. lunch break, meetings, while talking with your children . . .). Look for opportunities in the day to practise being open-minded. Then in the evening, review how your efforts have gone. Ask yourself if you have been able to suspend any of your previously held judgements to allow yourself to have a new experience today. Be careful not to judge your relative success or failure. Just try to notice how you were thinking throughout the day. That is enough.

We can learn something new from each situation in life.

Whether it is pleasant or difficult, planned or coincidental, an open mind offers abundant lessons, ideas or even wisdom. You might find yourself in a situation in which someone is stating ideas that are contrary to beliefs that you have long held. You might experience some event that contradicts all that you have before known to be true. Can you, for a moment, be open to the possibility of the correctness or truthfulness of this new experience or viewpoint? Instead of immediately passing judgement, can you take the time to pay attention, listen to this new situation and then further explore the experience, viewpoint or question at hand, to look into the details and assess them over time? Not that you have to make every or even any new idea your own. This would be quite dangerous. But can you create for yourself an inner, free space in which to live with a new or strange idea for a while before judging it, to see if it can prove its truthfulness to you?

In meeting with a new idea you can inwardly try to say, 'OH?' instead of, 'NO!' Let this new idea live in you as a question. It is possible that it will, in time, prove its value to you. Or equally, that evidence will mount to show you that this way of understanding things is not helpful. Nevertheless, the efforts of stretching your soul through the practice of open-mindedness will create a new faculty for discovery.

Focus on this exercise, as with the others, daily for a month. In time you might well notice a finer sensitivity to what your daily experiences bring to you and an enlivened openness to the wisdom of the world. This greater receptivity may well lead to new discoveries or intuitions that shed light on particular questions you are working with.

Notice in the two following anecdotes how the subjects

deal with their own previously held beliefs, how they are working or have been forced to work to overcome them. In the first you will read about one man's process of research into contemporary social issues. Having an open mind is an essential first step in his explorations. In the second you can see how a man, returning from a difficult visit to the doctor, had to overcome his notion of what being open-minded means, and stretch his thinking even further to discover new ways of being open not only to outer events, but also to the question of his own life or death.

Certain questions arise out of my interest and research into social life. I often take these questions out into the street and see where that leads me. I am interested in understanding the nature of what is work, why do people work and what is the correct way to see payment or compensation for their work.

I love walking in London and just being with people while carrying these questions in my thoughts. I remember once being at a train station, waiting for a train, which was late. I noticed one of the station staff sweeping the floor of the station platform. The way that he was sweeping might not have been considered particularly efficient. I found the situation interesting and tried to observe it carefully and objectively without any criticism or judgement. This objectivity and avoidance of any criticism was of fundamental importance if I wanted the situation to speak to my ongoing questions. I observed him carefully, to see every detail, with interest in who he was.

Quietly I asked to myself, 'Who are you? ... What is it to be you?'

But then I realized that I had already made two judgements, one was about the usual lateness of the trains and the other was about the inefficient quality of this man's sweeping. Any such criticisms, I knew, would be like a veil between this man, this situation and me. If I held onto these old ideas, I would not have been able to perceive why this man engaged in his work as he did, in which I was truly interested. I realized that it was only through judgement-free, deep compassion and interest that I would be able to come to some understanding of how this man related to his work.

Once I was able to get beyond these judgements, it was amazing how insight into the situation opened up for me. I found a deeper, fuller understanding of the connection between this human being, his work and the money he would receive as a wage. This new discovery was possible only because I was able to let go of previously held judgements and then to be completely open to the interest I felt for this man and his sweeping activity.

Financial Manager
Forest Row, England

I used to think that the challenge of being open-minded was to try to be open to people and events in the outside world. I have often practised being open to the views and opinions that other people have shared with me no matter how different they are from my own point of view. Recently, however, life has given me an opportunity to see open-mindedness from a whole new inner perspective.

I went to see the doctor for an exam. He found a solid tumour in my abdomen that might be cancerous. It would take a further examination to be sure whether it was benign or malignant.

My first reaction was interest and curiosity. But, I soon

realized that this could well be a life or death situation. It could be a harmless little growth that would in time go away or it could continue to grow and threaten my life. My thoughts were spinning out of control, first following one possibility that everything would be all right and then switching to the other possibility of my own, imminent death. Light and darkness, warmth and coldness, health and dying were chasing each other in my thoughts and throwing me completely out of balance. Anxiety and painful uncertainty tormented my mind. I had an inner openness only for life and for health. For the possibility of death, there was nothing but a painful cramping sensation.

A while later I sat down and told myself not to exclude the possibility of a difficult diagnosis, that I must be ready for this outcome too. At first this did not help. Then I took another step and told myself that I needed to cultivate openness to my higher self. It is far wiser than I am. Furthermore, I grew in confidence that whatever my higher self would decide would be the very best that could happen for my development. Still my thinking was raging and my emotions with it, too. But then there came another insight that trust in my higher self is what I most needed. I needed to learn how to be open to trusting divine guidance. Out of that trust I would gain the energy to be present in facing the challenge of pain, illness and even death. This realization helped me regain my equilibrium and to calm down. I was still under stress but trusted that no matter what happened it would serve that part of me which is here now and ever eternal.

It is now some months later and I have gratefully learned that the tumour was harmless. In retrospect I can see what a tremendous effort it has taken me to be open to impulses that come towards me from the inside. The whole experience of illness was essential to help me to be more open to my inner world, to cultivate trust in the unknown, both the unknown in me and in the eternal. This very quality of openness has helped me keep a better balance in my life even in the most challenging of circumstances.

Educational Researcher
Basel, Switzerland

7

Gratitude (Exercise 7)

Often life tests us through suffering,
leads us astray through joy;
so let us make joys the test of our heart
and sufferings paths to the truth.

Rudolf Steiner

Background to the exercise

The conscious cultivation of gratitude can transform all that has been developed so far in the first six exercises. Gratitude can become a positive force for change in the soul and in the world. By nurturing a fuller appreciation for other people and the events of life, gratitude can greatly enhance our personal development. Without all that others have contributed to our lives, we could not possibly be the people we are today. Beyond just our parents and grandparents, who have given us our bodies, homes and education, there are friends, teachers, bus drivers, cooks and a countless stream of other people who have touched our lives in innumerable ways. We are indebted to them for all that they have provided. The people who make light bulbs, printers of books, farmers and bakers have all contributed something essential to our lives, without which they would be very different.

We are indebted in the deepest way to the earth itself, to the plant life and to the animals as well as to the weather, the sun, and the planets beyond. They sustain the earth on whose

surface we dwell. From the tiniest grain of sand to the vast
expanse of the cosmos, we can come to acknowledge them
all with gratitude. All that is and has ever been allows that we
too may live, learn and have the opportunities to grow and to
help others. There can be no life without this vast web of
interconnections with all that has come before and all that has
yet to come. The past, present and future are all linked in a
vast web of gratitude.

In this spirit, I composed the following verse when I was
teaching the second grade (age 8) at the Waldorf School in
Olympia, Washington, USA. I created it to set the right
mood and rhythm to begin the day at school with my class of
18 students. Ostensibly, we used the verse to help us to pass
out a basket of beanbags around our circle. The rhythm of
the verse made this task much easier and turned it into a little
dance. The rhyming scheme made it easy to remember and
the substance of the verse wove together this deep sense for
mutual dependence and gratitude that can be at the heart of a
learning community.

> *We give the gift of joy and light,*
> *We pass it from our left to right.*
> *From friend to friend our hearts do reach,*
> *Around the circle each to each.*
>
> *To friend I give. From friend I get.*
> *We weave our caring friendship net.*
> *To give and get are one great deed.*
> *Our hearts and hands as one are freed.*

Around the circle the beanbags travelled from hand to hand,
effortlessly when all went well, but not when someone lost

the feel of the rhythm or was distracted. In learning, reciting and moving to this verse, each child could directly experience the essence of community, that each member formed an essential link in the circle of our class. The vitality of the whole depended on the efforts of each individual. Joy was evident in being able to harmonize our working together.

A community possesses all the gifts of its individual members as well as all of their shortcomings. Nevertheless, it is only through people trying to work in harmony with one another that the gifts of each one can fully emerge. A group can function at a higher (also lower) level than any one individual could on his or her own. It is really up to the conscious striving of the individuals involved.

Gratitude is a quality that truly connects us with all beings. 'In thankfulness all beings unite', concludes the poem 'Washing the Feet', by Christian Morgenstern. It is through a consciousness of gratitude that we can come to see how our lives are interdependent with all else that lives, in fact on all else that exists, has ever existed and will ever exist. And what is more, we (you and I) are essential aspects of this living and growing process. The world would not be any better without humans. We are an integral part of this whole. This is an opportunity to acknowledge the debt of connection that we owe to all beings, ourselves included. Here we have the possibility to see more fully our place in this world, to know where our responsibilities lie and to know how deeply we might touch the life of another person. Thus, our hearts and hands can be freed.

Furthermore, an active practice of cultivating gratitude is, in essence, a next step of harmonizing and balancing the first six exercises. An active practice in gratitude requires an open mind to all that has been positive or helpful in the day. It requires a balanced mood of equanimity, a strong will, clear thinking and an overview of the context of the whole day. The soul qualities developed in all six previous exercises come together within this last and most powerful one. This is the culmination of the series, and essentially contains them all.

The exercise is often people's favourite as it helps students to appreciate the immense generosity of others, intentionally given or not. The practice of cultivating gratitude can lead to more practical and effective ways of working in the world. It certainly will increase your sense of appreciation, your sense of awe and wonder for all the support your friends, family and colleagues give you. It will enliven your heart centre, or chakra, and will allow you to feel greater connections with other people and the world. It will give you greater insight into the innumerable ways in which people contribute to the lives of other people and, in fact, give them all opportunities for the growth that they are seeking.

Exercise 7: Gratitude

Celebrating specific instances for gratitude each day

There are many ways this exercise can be carried out. It can be the most creative of all of the seven exercises, as you can design your own variations. Basically the task is to take 5 to 10 minutes each day to think about how the actions of someone else have contributed to the betterment of your life in some way. You can do this at any time and might consider doing it immediately before you review your day.

Perhaps someone held a door open for you today, said a kind word, or smiled. Maybe an unexpected joy came your way or some simple regular task became enjoyable because of something unusual happening. It is also possible that someone gave you a challenge, a real difficulty, the facing of which brought new clarity, insight or strength to you. This could also be cause for gratitude. No gift can be either too small and common or too large or unusual to deserve to be noticed, and not only noticed but celebrated. This is a celebration of all the outer events that help us to grow and become the people we are. For we are shaped every bit as much by our inner character and destiny as we are by the outer events that play into our lives.

Simply picture inwardly (you may also want to write these down in your notebook) the scene in which this person or event affected your day. Imagine it as clearly as you can with as many of the details that you can call up from your memory. Notice the scene with all of its sensory details, what actually happened, how you initially received 'the gift' and how the gift grew or changed within you. Watch it clearly and then thank the person quietly in your mind. It is entirely possible that it could be an animal or a beautiful landscape as well, whose presence or smell touched you.

Whatever the case, think your gratitude and hold that thought for a minute or so. Then allow that thought of gratitude to build a warmth in the region of your heart. Imagine this warmth glowing, radiating from your heart. Then allow it to travel from your heart out through your arms and down your legs towards the heart of the other person or event you are remembering. This connection, while imagined, is also quite real. Do not underestimate the power of conscious thinking and feeling.

Recent scientific studies on the effects of prayer and healing of sick patients have shown that prayer (which can be another expression of gratitude) helps people to heal, even if they do not know that someone is praying for them. The effectiveness of prayer in promoting healing does not depend on the patient believing in the same religion or even in any religion at all. In other words, people definitely can perceive in some way (although rarely consciously) the thoughts of other people towards them. Thoughts have their own reality and existence once they are born in our minds. They do work in the world. While feelings of gratitude might well make your soul life richer, they will also enhance the well-being of those to whom they are directed. Try it for yourself.

If you like, you can also try to represent your gratitude in some other way. A friend of mine draws a picture of a flower for each person he thinks about. He draws the flower as a symbol of the gratitude he feels. He has no intention, however, of giving it to the other person. The drawing just aids his feelings and recognition for the deeds of the other person. Besides, he likes knowing that he has transformed his gratitude into action. It is not necessary, perhaps even detrimental, to give an actual gift or a physical acknowledgement. The warmth of your thinking has a much greater impact than might be imagined. A physical gift could stretch the exercise beyond a deepening of gratitude into the realm of wanting recognition or of feeling that you have to pay someone back for a kindness done to you. It would become an extreme burden to have to give back to everyone who has given to you. Rather, the focus of this exercise is on recognizing a few gifts each day in the complex web of interconnections that have helped you to become who and what you now are. Through this activity of acknowledging gifts to you, you become ever more aware of all that contributes to the lessons and meaning of your life.

If you do decide to give an actual gift, even a verbal thank-you to someone as a result of doing this exercise, take care in examining your motivation for doing so. There certainly is nothing wrong in giving gifts to others; just be aware why you are choosing to do so at this time. Is your thank-you seeking some sort of acknowledgement in return? If so then it would be best to refrain from giving an actual gift. A kind thought will do.

This is the last, culminating exercise in the sequence of seven. Steady and patient work will ultimately lead to the strengthening of your soul, your heart and your character. It will be impossible to practise them too often or too many times. Benefits will continue to flow to the most advanced student. It is the wisest people who realize just how much they still have to learn if they are to be of service to themselves, others and the physical and spiritual world. Patience will lead you one step at a time.

A teacher shared with me how this practice affected her life and how it might have been able to help to save another person in time of need. This is her story.

When times are difficult, I remind myself to 'Walk my Gratitude'. By this I mean to literally appreciate, with every step I am taking, all the help that I have received along the way as well as examples of beauty and goodness around me in the present moment. This past summer, as I was in the process of changing my career and moving to another country, I was feeling overwhelmed by all the details of what needed to be done. I felt so alone both in the decisions I had to make and in the work itself.

I sat down and made a list of all the people who had contributed to my move. It came to more than 30 people. Some I had paid. Others helped in small ways. But all of them together added up to a huge amount of support that made it all possible for me to take this new step in my life.

I then thought about a young man in my community who had committed suicide the week before. He had probably felt alone, really alone and without any help or recognition. He had completely given up hope and took his own life. I wondered how things might have gone differently if only he could have realized how much support he really had, and had known how many people truly felt connected with him.

Many people have come up to me during this period of many changes and have asked me how I was managing all these transitions so calmly. I realized that while I was not currently practising these exercises, they had in fact over many years become a part of me. By having cultivated equanimity, positivity, gratitude and having an open mind, these very ideals had become part of my character. I could not respond in any other way than with gratitude. I only wished that the young man had been able to see just how many people had cared about and for him too. It might have made all the difference for him.

Teacher
Boulder, USA

8

Along the Way: Obstacles and Progress

Outside ideas of right doing and wrong doing is a field. I'll meet you there.

Rumi

There are many factors that can support or impede your progress or sense of progress in pursuing this path. What follows is a discussion of some of the most common impediments and suggestions for how you might deal with and work towards overcoming them.

Plan ahead carefully and keep a notebook to mark your progress. It is not essential that you keep extensive notes but rather that you create as much clarity as possible for yourself. The notebook will help you to set out a plan and thus to know what you have decided to attempt each day. It can remind you of your original intentions and help you to hold yourself accountable. You can also note down any significant experiences that may have happened in the course of doing the exercises. Equally, other events might occur in your life that may affect what you are trying to achieve with these exercises. It is always good to write down whatever hindrances are keeping you from being as successful with the exercises as you would like to be. Then over time, you can see how your experiences are changing. Your notebook is a historical learning tool and a great aid in staying focused on what you have set out to do.

There are some common obstacles which many people experience along their paths of inner development. While at times they feel annoying or frustrating, they can also be viewed as teachers, helping you to see the dynamics of your own inner processes. Each time one of them emerges into your thinking or hinders your fullest engagement in performing these exercises, it is as if a hidden part of your character has revealed itself for your information, examination and, ultimately, for your benefit. This is an opportunity to recognize and begin to appreciate those parts of your character that have defined and limited your awareness until now. By acknowledging them and thanking them for sharing their point of view, you can begin to liberate yourself from their exclusive perspective. Thus a more objective picture of you in your environment can emerge as you see that the obstacle is just presenting you with one of your accustomed ways of perceiving the world.

Let us take a look now at some of these more common challenges that so many people on a path of self-development have encountered. While working through them can be frustrating, it is possible to relate to them with a sense of lightness and even humour. They are, after all, our teachers.

The inner critic

The inner critic cruelly judges all that we do. It can say terrible things to us like: 'You are not doing this exercise very well! You missed another essential detail! You are stupid! You are lazy! You have just fallen asleep again, dummy! Why don't you just give up now because you'll never be any good at this!'

The inner critic reflects our highest strivings in their lowest forms. In its incessant and often debasing vocabulary, the inner critic measures us against our highest ideals for our behaviour and for that of all people in general. It is only by holding these very high ideals within ourselves that we can hope to grow and develop as human beings. But we should be careful not to allow our inner critic to twist these ideals into severe criticisms that, in effect, actually stifle our initiative. It could easily happen that someone feels paralysed by this strident voice of criticism. Befriend it, and it will serve you. Fight it, and it will rebuff your efforts. This is your choice with any challenge that life offers. With the right attitude, anything can become your teacher.

Neither young children nor animals seem to suffer at the hands of self-criticism. Their consciousness is immune to the inner critic. They do not measure themselves by the same standards as do adult humans and do not have this same level of inner dialogue. The inner critic no matter how terrible it seems nevertheless has much to teach us if we can adjust our relationship to it. It can reveal to us our highest aims in life. It definitely wants us to be more than we currently are, to be better, brighter, more compassionate and/or more successful. If we can learn to listen to its message with a little more discretion, it can point us to a more fruitful future.

In changing this relationship the first step is to translate everything the inner critic tells us into the positive aim or ideal that lies behind its language. 'You are so foolish!' can

become, 'I wish that I felt more intelligent.' Taken a step
further, this can be transformed into an impetus for action,
such as, 'I would like to cultivate my intelligence. Maybe I'll
read a book or take a class.' As your friend or ally, the critic
can point you in the right direction. It might even give you
an indication of the next exercise that you would like to be
doing once you translate its critical language into more
appropriate and life-affirming language.

When you are engaging in these exercises, and the inner
critic interrupts you with an insight, try to receive it neutrally
no matter how cruel the message might be. Thank the critic
for all he tries to offer and let him go his way. And by all
means do not believe what he has to say verbatim. The more
you are able to thank him, acknowledge his aim and then
send him on his way, the less his familiar opinions will tarnish
your days. In wrestling with him, new strength can develop
within you, strength and courage to see yourself more clearly
and honestly.

The inner chatter

The chatterer similarly wants your attention. He has all these
(not-so-important) things he wants to tell you NOW.
Endless lists and litanies of stuff that he wants to bring before
your mind's eye, and patience is not his gift. So he butts into
your every activity and blurts out whatever is on his mind.
He says the least important things at the least helpful or
appropriate times. Why would you need to think about your
car for instance while trying to focus on thinking about a

pencil, or the shopping list or what you did last Sunday? These distractions do not enrich the activity in which you are currently trying to engage.

The best way to deal with the chatterer is similar to dealing with the inner critic; simply thank him for sharing and let him go. He will of course continue to visit, but the more often you receive him calmly, acknowledge him, thank him and let him go, the fewer demands he will make on your attention. You will become better able to focus on what you are presently doing. You may come to owe a tremendous debt of gratitude to the interruptions of the chatterer. He can help you to appreciate and cultivate inner calm and quiet as well as focused activity. So whenever he visits, you can welcome him as an old and familiar friend and ally. Thank him, and off he'll go. Gradually you can begin to be the master of what thoughts, images and feelings stand before your mind's eye.

Neither of these two voices are you. They merely emerge in your mind and sound in you. You are the consciousness that is aware of them. Your higher consciousness or higher self is that part of you that can be aware of all the other impulses in your soul. This higher self is the aspect of your being that you will come to know and appreciate more and more in the course of your inner development. You can either listen to your higher self or to these lesser voices, the inner critic and chatterer. But to begin to see your identity as separate from their distracting messages is most helpful. Once you do so, you will find many of your former limitations lift and you feel much freer to express yourself and do what you most wish.

Discouragement

Of course, even without the presence of the inner critic or the chatterer, these exercises can be challenging to do each and every day. Sometimes it can feel that your progress has either slowed to a halt or that it is completely impossible to succeed at a particular exercise, and you feel discouraged. The first step when this happens is to look at the plan that you made for your practice of this series of exercises. Is it a realistic plan? Does it take into account the other responsibilities that you must also manage in your daily life? If not, then it would be best to reconsider the challenges that you have set for yourself and to redesign your schedule so that you can actually achieve what you set out to do. Maybe it will be necessary to do a little less. It is far more strengthening to build from success than to have to pick yourself up from failure.

Another discouraging experience is feeling that your progress is slowing down or has come to a complete halt. You may feel concern that your abilities are even decreasing or weakening at times. This is common, as the learning curve is never linear. Sometimes your improvement will slow down naturally. At other times it will stall altogether, or seem to go backwards. Just be patient and tolerant with yourself and know that with continued practice you will continue to progress. Nothing can replace the empowering combination of steady preparation and patience.

It is also common for people to feel that some exercises are more difficult for them than others. This is natural and indicates an area or skill in need of more attention. It is the difficult exercises that might well need your attention most. In a very real way, they have the most to teach you. Nevertheless, use your own discretion to simplify an exercise if needed, so that you can build that capacity stepwise. There is little point in pushing yourself to the point of frustration or failure. If the Review of the Day exercise, for example, is too difficult for you to complete for the whole day, review some smaller segment of your day. While it would be ideal to look back over your day from the time you went to bed in the evening to the time you awoke from sleep in the morning, for many people this is too difficult. Likewise, if you are having difficulty doing the Positive World View exercise throughout the entire day, then focus on a narrower window of time or even on a single experience. This will allow you to better focus your energies and to experience more success.

Try not to skip an exercise or stay fixed on any one for too long a time, especially when you are attempting these for the first time, as this will detract from their harmonizing, mutually enhancing effect. Keep in mind that these exercises are designed to balance your soul development. It is most effective to do all seven in the sequence given the first time you work with them. While these exercises are completely safe, experience shows that healthy development comes from practising all of them sequentially and then in various arrangements, say exercises 2 and 3, then exercises 4 and 5, or exercises 2 and 5 and then exercises 3 and 6. I also urge you to continue the first exercise, the Review of the Day, as part of your daily, personal practice. No matter what other exercises or meditations you are doing, the Review of the Day will always be helpful in digesting the gifts of the day. Also, remember that this is not called practice and exercise for nothing. It takes some doing. The rewards, while subtle, can be significant and life-enhancing.

Boredom

On the other hand, the opposite problem that some people experience while doing these exercises is boredom. If you get bored, you are probably not giving yourself enough of a challenge. Push yourself to make the exercises a bit more difficult. Either do them for a longer period of time or be more specific in the details of the exercises. Ask yourself, 'Could I be more conscious of how I am carrying out this challenge?' I have practised many different Intention in Action exercises, two of them for over three years, and still found it rewarding and beneficial. I challenged myself every day at a specific time to take my watch out of my pocket, pass it around my body and then put it back in my pocket again. This soon became the most enjoyable meaningless task that I have ever done! Even if I was in the middle of a meeting, in a shop or on an aeroplane, I still tried to remember my watch at the same time and to do it so discreetly that no one else would know that I was doing an exercise. I felt satisfaction and challenge in doing it no matter what the outer circumstances of my life were. Sometimes I laughed at myself at doing such a silly thing with such commitment. Once the challenge became a bit easier and I could do it most days, I would challenge myself to see how many days in a row I could do it. This turned it into a little game that I played with myself. It became one of my day's simple pleasures.

A man who has worked with these exercises over many decades spent 20 years contemplating the same pair of wooden chopsticks in the Cultivation of Thinking exercise. Each day he found something new, something interesting in these seemingly simple objects. The chopsticks did not change over the years, but his openness and interest in them evolved throughout his practice in a way that allowed him to be more open and interested in many other phenomena. It built his basic ability to find interest in something, thus making the possibility of boredom more remote.

There is plenty to explore in each exercise for a lifetime or more. If you run out of ideas, ask a teacher or a friend for new ones. Even the most advanced practitioners have much to learn and maintain in their souls by doing these basic exercises. And if you choose to go on to another form of meditation, these exercises are an excellent complement to any path of inner learning. They will help keep you grounded and in balance, while also developing sensitivity for the subtle abilities of your soul.

Unable to find a rhythm—busy or irregular life

Success in carrying out these seven exercises is all about rhythm: creating an inner rhythm in your life to support the development of new capacities or the strengthening of existing ones. Remember the old maxim 'Rhythm replaces strength'! A healthy rhythm will lead to harmonious long-term soul development. Schedule your practice so that it fits in with the natural rhythms of your life and your responsibilities. Keep in mind that it will take seven months to complete the entire sequence of exercises, after which time a short break is recommended before repeating the whole sequence again. This will also cultivate patience and protect you from pride. In fact, simply creating this type of life-affirming rhythm in your life can be one immediate benefit of doing these exercises. A healthy rhythm can make work into dance and speech into song. That is why in former times people sang while they worked. The rhythm made the work lighter and made the task go more quickly and pleasurably.

Breathing and posture

Unlike practices in yoga, a specific physical posture and type of breathing are not central to the practice of these exercises. These exercises are designed to cultivate new and balanced capacities for your soul, which is connected to but also distinct from your physical constitution. While your physical body and soul are intimately connected and interdependent, these exercises focus on soul development and are best practised in a way that is independent of any particular physical posture or specific breathing pattern. I suggest you focus your attention not so much on body posture or breathing but on the challenge of the exercise itself. Find a place, where you are least likely be interrupted and a posture that is relaxed and comfortable for you. As stated earlier, there are a variety of postures in which people successfully do their practices. Some people prefer to sit in a chair or at its edge, others sit on the floor, lie down in bed or even stand up. Choose the posture and environment that most supports your capacity to focus on your practice, and breathe naturally. You may find, in fact, that the exercises affect your breathing, calming and slowing it, rather than the other way round.

Temperature and appropriate clothing can also be important in maintaining your focus on the exercises. Dress comfortably and warmly, but do not get so comfortable that you are likely to fall asleep. And if you do fall asleep, try to continue with the exercise when you wake up, from where you left off. It is never too late to try again or to improve.

Physical or emotional stress

In times of physical or emotional stress you may find it difficult to stay focused on your original plan for doing the exercises. The chatterer and the inner critic may well be talking non-stop and every other hindrance may creep in as a confirmation of the level of your stress. If this happens, then ask yourself if it would be possible to keep to your rhythm but change your expectations. Instead of focusing for 15 minutes, would it be possible to continue for just a minute or two a day? Try that. You may well find that the effort needed to do a minute easily stretches into 5 or even 15 minutes anyway. Consistency is the important thing. This continuity can give you strength in times of difficulty as well as plant the seeds for your long-term development. It is surprising that when all else is failing around you these simple exercises can be a source of great strength. They may, in fact, be all that keeps you from swirling in the whirlpool of your emotions. Do your best and have patience with yourself. Let your practice become a source of certainty in the rhythm of your life. As you have read in many of the anecdotes, these practices can have a tremendously grounding and sustaining effect on people in times of need.

Interruptions

Less dramatic, but perhaps likely to happen more often are the small (or not so small) interruptions to your practice of these exercises. It could be a child wanting your attention, a knock on the door or an important telephone call. It would be best if you could carve out your times so that the inner work takes priority over other demands. However, this is not always possible. If you cannot delay responding to an interruption until after you have completed your task at hand, then it is best to consciously stop working on the exercises for that session. Be conscious that you are ending your session early. Then, if you think you may be able to, make a date with yourself for later in the day in order to continue with the exercises where you had to leave off.

With your exercise session clearly over, you will be better able to give your full attention to the interruption that could not wait. You can aspire to be fully present in the moment, just as you are trying to be fully present in doing your exercises. The exercises, after all, should not be separated from life. Presence is the essence of giving your full attention to one thing at a time. You will soon find that not only do you perform tasks better, but that you also feel much more satisfaction from doing so. And most likely, you will be able to accomplish a whole lot more.

Travelling or visitors

Travelling or having people visiting you can also add a challenge to keeping with the rhythm of your original plan of practice. As much as is possible, try to find opportunities to stick with your rhythm even if you have to shorten the exercises or do them in a very different manner, for instance in a meeting or on an aeroplane. Take this as an opportunity to be creative. Find a way to do your exercises in a new or different way. I can remember faithfully doing another Intention in Action exercise every day for over three years (walking backwards in a circle three times). This was a unique challenge on a cross-country train trip that I happened to be on. However, finding a way to do it at the allotted time was as fulfilling as it was entertaining. Meeting the challenge without drawing undue attention to myself certainly made the train ride a lot more interesting.

Falling asleep

When a day has been full or you have waited until too late in the evening to try your exercises, it can often happen that you fall asleep while doing them. For many people it can be such a challenge to make it all the way through the Review of the Day, especially if the demands of the day have left them with little extra energy. At these times, a sitting or even standing posture can be better than trying to do your review while lying in bed. Use whatever position or environment helps you to stay focused and alert, as well as reasonably comfortable.

Sometimes you may realize well before the end of the day that you will be just too tired to do the whole routine well. In this situation, try to find time in your schedule for your practice earlier in the day. Give yourself every chance of succeeding. Do your exercises when you have the most energy and greatest focus. If it does happen that you know that you cannot perform the exercises as well as you would like, then decide (best if before you begin) to do a shorter version of your routine. At least by doing a shortened version, you maintain the steady rhythm of daily practice. This, in and of itself, can be beneficial for your continued soul development.

In this next anecdote observe how the person overcomes his feelings of frustration, confusion and discouragement while doing one of the exercises. He has a creative and insightful approach to integrating this work with the rigours of his life.

My problem with the exercise for cultivating clear thinking is that the clarity and precision of my thought processes persist only within the realm of what I can be confident that I know. As I approach the boundary of what I actually know for sure, my thinking becomes less certain and diffuse. No longer am I practising clear, steady thinking; rather, as I approach the limits of my real understanding, my process shifts to that of actively wondering and honestly questioning. In many ways, this seems like a healthy, natural part of an honest thought process or investigation: recognizing what is known, and recognizing what is unknown. But what percentage of my time in practising this exercise should include the crafting of honest and accurate questions? And how much time should I spend affirming my ignorance by wondering at questions for which a little research could easily supply clear answers?

For example: I consider a sewing needle. I examine its size and shape. I relate these qualities to its use, and relate the use to the needs of the user. I consider the modern sewing needle, and the way its regularity and fineness allow people to make neat and durable clothing. I think about the origin of sewing needles: awls, animal skin and plant fibre cordage sewn with large, clunky bone needles.

But there is a break at this point. I do not truly know how sewing needles (thread and sewing) evolved from bone. I can conjecture. But to me, the process of guessing at the particulars of how sewing needles developed from bone to metal feels contrary to my purpose in this exercise. And so, I begin asking clear questions: When did metal sewing needles first appear? What type of metal were they made of? How were they made? How are modern sewing needles made? What types of metal are they made from?

This was typical of my practice of the thought exercise for a while. But then I was enlightened by the idea of researching about the simple object as a background and foundation for the thought exercise. It seemed like an easy way to mend the unsatisfying aspect of my practice. I went to the library, and looked up sewing needles in an encyclopaedia. I found two pages of real answers to most of my questions, including an in-depth description of the 20 distinct manufacturing processes that make modern sewing needles from a coil of wire.

That evening my thought exercise was focused, ordered, undistracted and sure. How satisfying! I still had many questions, of course. But these questions seemed like natural extensions of my real knowing; and, the proportion of understanding to questioning was such that my practice felt like an exercise of thinking instead of an exercise of wondering.

I continue to choose objects at random, without researching them in advance. This way, I develop my own questions through my own thought processes. And then, at a time that seems natural to me, I seek answers to my mounting questions. And so my process of practising the thought exercise is much like my process of engaging with meditation, as well as engaging in the world through active living: never-ending questions to be wondered at and explored through life.

Community Activist
Olympia, Washington, USA

9

Harmonizing Intentions

The reason the earth lies shattered and in pieces is because man is disunited from himself . . .

Ralph Waldo Emerson

It is time, as Emerson urges, to find all these shattered pieces, pick them up and recreate our world anew. These seven exercises are an effective first step towards reuniting the fragments, helping us to reunite with the essence of who we really are and what we would most like to bring to the world. The effort of attempting and doing these exercises supports our inner development, which is necessary for any real progress to occur. By practising them in the sequence given and then in all of their various possible combinations and permutations, they can lead to dynamic and healthy soul development. Together, they form a whole, leading to balanced and consistent growth for anyone at any stage of his or her journey. This growth is important both for our own individual soul development and to support the efforts of others to evolve. Our personal development can become a positive force for social change.

Some of my students have pointed out with some astonishment that even though the second exercise, cultivation of thinking, is about taking control of and strengthening your thinking, actually doing the exercise on a regular basis takes a tremendous amount of *will*. It is hard to commit to and persist with focusing your thinking on a simple object for a period of time every day. It takes a tremendous effort over many days just to do it, let alone to do it consistently well. Not only is it a challenge for the will, but maintaining your equilibrium between interest, boredom, pride and self-criticism is an immense effort of balancing your feeling life as well. This requires a deep cultivation of equanimity, so that your feeling life supports what you are trying to do with your thinking and your will. Thus, while this exercise is supposed to be about controlling your capacity and focus in thinking, thinking itself never exists in a vacuum, but is always interconnected with feelings and will impulses. The cultivation of any one of them automatically demands the cultivation of the others.

As an integral series of exercises, these seven exercises nurture the entire human being in a balanced and life-affirming way, giving each aspect an opportunity to blossom in harmony with all your other capacities. The following diagram shows the dynamic ways in which these exercises support one another in helping to cultivate balanced soul development.

These seven exercises progress in a geometrically harmonious manner. The Review of the Day establishes fuller
awareness of all that touches the soul each day. It lays the
foundation of attention and intention upon which the others
can work more fruitfully. Then come the next three exercises, Clear Thinking, Intention in Action and Balance in
Feeling. These complete the first upward-pointing triangle
and strengthen each of the three basic soul activities, thinking, feeling and will. They form the stable base upon which
the remaining three exercises can bring your soul into harmonious balance.

Positive World View lies across from Balance in Feeling,
because it is, in a sense, this exercise raised to the next level.
Beyond cultivating equanimity, the Positive World View
exercise encourages you to strive to use your feeling for the
positive as a creative tool. It harnesses the creative potential of
your inner life of feelings. Open Mind is placed across from
Clear Thinking as it stretches your linear, logical thinking
into ever broader circles of interest, attention and understanding. Through the practice of Open Mind, your clear
logical thinking can grow to embrace new concepts with
absolute certainty and conviction. Thinking can become a
true tool for knowing.

Gratitude marks the culmination of these exercises. Placed
opposite to Intention in Action, a true act, or expression, of
gratitude is one of the highest forms of the will, of the force of
love itself. It is a deed that keeps on giving both to the giver
and to the recipient. In gratitude all beings unite. Thus
Positive World View, Open Mind and Gratitude form a
complementary triangle which inverted above the other one

(of Clear Thinking, Balance in Feeling and Intention in Action) gives the resulting six-pointed star, a stable harmony between earth and heaven, male and female principles joined in a lasting union. Looked at in this way, these exercises strengthen and transform various soul capacities into a dynamic and yet stable equilibrium. Each one cultivates the soul in a health-giving, mutually enhancing and life-affirming way.

I would like to stress one final time the importance of doing all the exercises in the order here given from start to finish. If you do not feel that you can commit yourself to attempting all of them, then it might be better to wait for a more auspicious moment to begin. Personal development that takes a student further away from an inner sense of balance than at the outset can be less helpful than not embarking on this path at all. As an example, I am sure we all know people who seem to act before they think, whose emotions always seem to get the better of them, or others who seem to be stuck in their heads, thinking more than is healthy for them. These are the possible and undesired consequences of one-sided development, of having any one of these capacities so well developed that it dominates the others.

Here is an account written by a man who has managed to find rhythm and meaning in his life by finding a balanced practice of bicycle riding and composing haiku poetry. He exercises both body and soul in quiet inner mindfulness. While it is an unusual path, it speaks of the benefits of inventiveness and perseverance. The essence of these exercises can grow with you and fit into whatever lifestyle you have chosen.

Being autumn, it is still dark as I bicycle down the hills away from my home, passing just a couple of cars. On most mornings, I see few. Leaving the apartment buildings and traffic lights behind, I feel a sense of calmness, relaxation and freedom as the visual and audio stimuli become less invasive and imposing. Now small farms, houses and mountains surround me. The road is not level or straight, yet it is basically flat.

The smell of rice nearing harvest overwhelms me. This and the brilliant and clear night sky are what interest me this morning, and I try to focus on these two images and transform them into a traditional haiku, 5 syllables–7 syllables–5 syllables. I consider various words, combinations and orders. Those that seem fruitful, I try to hold in memory. Over and over again, back and forth, contemplating wording and syllable count, my mind searches around and zooms in.

On other days, I try to create something in narrative out of what I centre my attention on, or perhaps I hold onto an image that is more visually stunning for later artistic interpretation. On other mornings, I set out with a thought to ponder already in mind. Or I may search for things which make today different than yesterday, or that make it typical of the season.

Of course, I cannot completely forget that I am bicycling. My legs must continue to peddle, with varying strength. I must still have some of my attention directed to the road and to other things and beings that might be on it. My hands must be ready to react immediately if necessary. Some of this is now unconscious after many years of this routine, but I must always keep some conscious awareness of what I am doing and what is going on around me regardless of what I am contemplating and feeling.

After turning around, I go back the way I came. I ride the same route every day. This is so my body and perception have better chances of knowing what they will need to do and will encounter. This allows me to have more freedom and to develop more inner sensitivity and depth in my feeling and thinking. They are not constantly facing something new or different. It also forces me to view and experience my surroundings in more detail, as I pass the same places every time I ride. In the east, dawn is now turning the sky a light orangey-pink.

As I begin to climb up the hills back to my home, I need to allot more of my concentration for my pedalling, and it takes more effort to hold onto any thoughts or images I want to keep from the morning's experiences. Day after day, week after week, year after year, I have been rising in the wee hours of the morning to do this for myself, not every single day, but most days and regularly. Allocating time for myself is a first step for any kind of exercise, physical or mental, as is the will to do it over and over again patiently and repeatedly.

brightly shining stars
the smell of ripening rice
ever pervasive

Teacher
Kobe, Japan

10

What is the Soul?

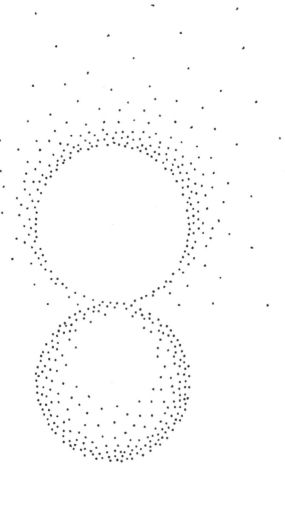

The first step in seeking happiness is learning. We first have to learn how negative emotions and behaviours are harmful to us, and how positive emotions and behaviours are helpful. And we must realize how these negative emotions are not only very bad and harmful to one personally but harmful to society and the future of the whole world as well. That kind of realization enhances our determination to face and overcome them.

His Holiness the Dalai Lama

It may seem strange to address this question at the end of the book, when soul development is the essential focus of the exercises, and therefore closely connected with the very nature and definition of the soul. However, I regard questions of belief or non-belief—which debate about the soul inevitably involves—as secondary to the practice described here. These exercises can have a powerful effect whatever one believes the soul to be.

The word 'soul' has a long and somewhat confusing history. It has been used in a great variety of ways and with many different meanings. It has been connected variously with the spirit, thinking, the physical senses and also a sense of morality. Charles Dickens once said, 'The absence of the soul is far more terrible in a living man than in a dead one.' Soul seems integral to our humanity. To be without soul is to be soulless (i.e. immoral) or a zombie. Yet questions of the substance of the soul, how it is connected or related to the physical body and what becomes of the soul after death have been much debated.

Over the last 2500 years, the soul has most often been regarded as a synonym for the spirit or the eternal aspect of each human being, for the part of us that continues to exist beyond death. The spirit/soul lives for ever while the earthly body decays back to dust. According to the Greek philosopher Plato, the soul is demonstrably immortal and imperishable. It is the seat of each person's individuality, the fount out of which pours the qualities of each person's character. Aristotle, his student, argued that the soul is the 'essential whatness of a being' that is present when a body is alive. It is connected with both the senses and the ability to think, remember and reason. He countered, however, that the immortality of the soul could not be observed or proven, that the soul can be perceived in the body, but does not appear to have a separate existence.

The founders of the early Christian church described the soul in differing ways as that part of the human being that connects the physical body with the eternal, divine spirit. St Augustine claimed that the natural action of the soul is to search for truth. He held that through exercising self-examination, the soul attains pure reason and union with the divine.

More recent thinkers, however, such as Immanuel Kant, have claimed that the soul does not exist at all in its own right, but that it is only an intellectual concept of human invention, created to deal with fears of death and decay. As its existence cannot be proven, its independent and immortal characteristics are left in doubt. Materialistic thinkers go further and assert that the human organism is solely (and soullessly) a genetically driven, biochemical reaction with no need for an old-fashioned concept like the soul. The soul simply does not exist. It, like God, is an unnecessary construct.

I do not intend to enter into the debate on the immortality of each person's human essence, but it is only fair to acknowledge that for this author the word soul denotes a reality that underpins the exercises described in this book. The soul, in my view, while distinct from the spirit, is not a figment of the imagination, an empty word for a fictitious concept.

What do I mean by soul? First of all, casual observation shows that you are more than just a physical body that is at present sitting and reading this book. You have a name, an identity with a memory, interests, passions, a personal history as well as intentions or hopes for the future. You have the ability to think, feel and act. Besides the physical substance of your body, you also have an awareness of past, present and future, a whole inner and interconnected world. You attend to relationships with other people, process sensory impressions and have to some degree (for better or for worse) an awareness or consciousness of self. You experience a whole range of thoughts, emotions and impulses to do things. Each tells you something about yourself and your situation in life.

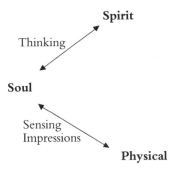

The soul serves as a connecting bridge between the 'I Am'—our essential identity, higher self, spirit—and our physical body in the physical world which we inhabit, with our physical senses. It is the mediator between these two very different aspects of self and the world and, as such, has elements of each within it. Without the existence of the soul, the body and spirit/mind would be divided from each another, as Descartes in fact posited. The soul bridges these opposites, thus enabling us to be aware of the world, of other people and, uniquely for human beings, to be self-aware.

The soul can be viewed as having three main aspects, broadly denoted by the terms feeling, thinking and action. Firstly it has a sensing, feeling ability that allows us to perceive the state of things both outside and inside ourselves. It produces either a feeling of sympathy (an attraction and desire for union with the perception) or a feeling of antipathy (a repulsion or desire for separation from the perception). Secondly, the soul allows us to reflect upon and think about what our senses and feelings have made available to us and to compare this with ideas that we previously held. Thirdly, the soul translates our thoughts and feelings into purposeful action.

Properties of the soul, mediating between self and world

1. Feeling/perceiving sensory impressions (inner and outer).
2. Thinking about, comparing and understanding sense impressions.
3. Acting upon these feelings and thoughts.

The soul referred to in this book is an active, dynamic organization of these three interrelating capacities that form the essential link between inner self, feelings, thoughts, impulses, desires and outer deeds. It is these same soul capacities that I seek to identify, clarify and strengthen through the exercises presented in this book.

It should be noted that animals also have souls, but that they function differently from human souls. Animal souls live in a detailed awareness of the outside world, to a much more refined degree than human awareness of the environment. A dog's sense of smell or an eagle's ability to see is far more sensitive than ours, allowing decisive, instinctive behaviour and immediate and predictable responses. An animal soul, however, is less suited to self-reflective awareness or to thinking about anything other than perceptions. It is less individual than a human soul. A lion, for instance, can never act like a peacock, but a human being can act in ways reminiscent of, say, a lion, a peacock, cow or giraffe. Animals are more fixed in their relationship to their physical form and to the environment in which they live. Humans can live almost anywhere on the planet, and even beyond for short periods of time.

This image of the human soul with its three distinct capacities can facilitate a detailed understanding of the dynamic nature of human awareness, emotion and activity. A clearer picture of the human soul can help you to find ways to nurture your many soul capacities. You can educate your soul and help it to develop in manifold ways, which can enrich any aspect of your personal, professional or public life. This striving can help you to do even ordinary things extra-ordinarily well.

Appendix 1: Plan of Action

The following proposed schedule is a way of fruitfully working with the exercises. It allows you to focus on one new exercise each month while continuing to practise the exercises that you have already learned the previous month. Give priority and focus to learning the newest exercise. Nevertheless, continue to practise the older exercises so that you can help them deepen and mature in your soul. This will reinforce the harmonizing properties of the whole programme.

First month	Review of the Day	5 to 20 minutes in the evening
Second month	Review of the Day	5 to 15 minutes in the evening
	Clear Thinking	5 minutes in the morning
Third month	Review of the Day	5 to 15 minutes in the evening
	Clear Thinking	5 minutes in the morning
	Intention in Action	at specific time(s) in the day
Fourth month	Review of the Day	5 to 15 minutes in the evening
	Clear Thinking	5 minutes in the morning
	Intention in Action	at specific time(s) in the day
	Balance in Feeling	throughout the day

Fifth month	Review of the Day	5 to 15 minutes in the evening
	Clear Thinking	5 minutes in the morning
	Intention in Action	at specific time(s) in the day
	Balance in Feeling	throughout the day
	Positive World View	throughout the day
Sixth month	Review of the Day	5 to 15 minutes in the evening
	Clear Thinking	5 minutes in the morning
	Intention in Action	at specific time(s) in the day
	Balance in Feeling	throughout the day
	Positive World View	throughout the day
	Open Mind	throughout the day
Seventh month	Review of the Day	5 to 15 minutes in the evening
	Clear Thinking	5 minutes in the morning
	Intention in Action	at specific time(s) in the day
	Balance in Feeling	throughout the day
	Positive World View	throughout the day
	Open Mind	throughout the day
	Gratitude	5 minutes in the evening or morning

After completing this cycle of seven months I suggest you take a brief break to take stock of the work you have done and the changes you have observed. When you are ready, continue to practise all of these exercises in various combinations (i.e. 1 and 3, 2 and 4, etc.) or begin the entire sequence again. Try to work with the ones that are most challenging for you.

Appendix 2: Further Thoughts

I would like to accentuate the fact that these exercises should not draw you out of the stream of your daily responsibilities or duties but rather should give you the tools for becoming more effective in all that you set out to do. The intention is not to give you so many exercises that the responsibilities of your daily life suffer in consequence. These exercises will enhance the reality of everyday life, not supplant it. They will help create an open space within yourself so that you can have the patience to respond to a situation creatively rather than only reacting to it.

In his lectures and writings Rudolf Steiner repeatedly emphasizes the importance of Exercise 1, Review of the Day. While he is not the originator of this exercise, Steiner stressed time and again that this is the most important exercise for anyone interested in self-development to practise. The following quote is taken from *An Outline of Occult Science:*

> The ability to behold one's own experiences, one's own joys and sorrows as though they were the joys and sorrows of others is a good preparation for spiritual training. One gradually attains the necessary degree of this quality if, after one has finished one's daily tasks, one permits the panorama of one's daily experiences to pass before the eyes of the spirit. One must see oneself in a picture within one's experiences; that is, one must observe oneself in one's daily life as though from outside. One attains a certain ability in such self-

observation if one begins with the visualization of
detached portions of this daily life. One then becomes
increasingly clever and skilful in such retrospect, so that,
after a longer period of practice, one will be able to
form a complete picture within a brief span of time.
This looking at one's experiences backward has a special
value for spiritual training for the reason that it brings
the soul to a point where it is able to release itself in
thinking from the previous habit of merely following in
thought the course of everyday events. In thought-
retrospect one visualizes correctly, but one is not held to
the sensory course of events. One needs this exercise to
familiarize oneself with the spiritual world. [Page 291*]

Exercises 2 through 7 have been cultivated from material
given by Rudolf Steiner in this same book. Through personally practising these exercises over many years as well as
teaching and practising them with students at Emerson
College, I have sought to make them as understandable as
possible and thus fruitful to work with. In any effort towards
clarity, and translation into a more modern idiom, there is a
risk of losing some of the essence of the original. Therefore, I
would like to offer a further quote from Chapter 5 of this
same book to give interested readers a feeling for the flavour
of the original:

In a factual training certain qualities are mentioned that
the student who wishes to find his way into the higher
worlds should acquire through practice. These are,

---

*Rudolf Steiner, *An Outline of Occult Science*, translated by M. & H.
Monges, Anthroposophic Press, Spring Valley 1972.

above all, control of the soul over its train of thought, over its will, and its feelings. The way in which this control is to be acquired through practice has a twofold purpose. On the one hand, the soul is to be imbued with firmness, certainty and equilibrium to such a degree that it preserves these qualities, although from its being a second ego is born. On the other hand, this second ego is to be furnished with strength and inner consistency of character...

What is necessary for the thinking of man in spiritual training is, above all, objectivity. In the physical sensory-world, life is the human ego's great teacher of objectivity. [Page 283]

These passages clearly show that such practices form the foundation for seeking further knowledge in the world of spirit. Beyond just strengthening the soul for the trials of daily life, they are also an essential foundation for developing meditative practice. Yet this step is left to the initiative of each individual in complete freedom. Doing these exercises does not in any way compel one to engage in a meditative practice. Should this be your interest or desire, however, Appendix 3 addresses the topic of meditation.

Appendix 3:
Developing a Daily Practice in Meditation

Meditation is derived from the Greek word *Medomai*, which means to 'think about'. But its meaning has shifted in modern usage to include not only regular thought and contemplation (i.e. to meditate on a problem one is experiencing) but also more devotional or religious states of focused attention. In this case, a practitioner (or meditant) could be said to be sitting in meditation as part of a daily practice of meditation. But sitting meditation is only one amongst many paths of harnessing this inner quality or deeper level of connection.

There are countless ways to focus your attention or meditate, which come from both the eastern and the western hemispheres. These are often called schools or paths of meditation. The ancient traditions of Yoga, Buddhism, Jewish Cabbala and esoteric Christianity, for example, have all developed exercises designed to strengthen and cultivate particular qualities. Each in turn has developed a language to describe a person's relationship with the higher self, spirit or God. There are also many modern teachers and schools, often deriving their teachings from these older sources of wisdom. They offer their own particular path for deepening connection with the self, the world, God and/ or the 'higher self'. Each school of meditation has its own particular approach or discipline and offers the possibility of developing different aspects of an enriched inner life. Some paths emphasize concentrating on the breathing and/or putting one's body in particular postures. Some require physical hardship and the renunciation of certain physical pleasures. Others focus on clearing the mind of all content and entering fully into that calm inner space. And still other schools emphasize putting specific content before the mind's eye and contemplating on its essence. This content could be in the form of a natural object, a sound, a mantric verse, a mental image or a specific thought construct. What all require is a calmness of mind and a stillness of body so that deeper states of consciousness can be achieved. The mind and body must be quietened so that the student can become aware of more subtle, non-physical sensations and influences, and connect with the divine.

Each is a unique movement or school in itself, and it is well beyond the scope of this book to describe each one in a more detailed manner, or to compare one path with another. Nevertheless, these schools have many attributes in common, and can in many ways be seen as part of a larger picture of the development of human consciousness. They address the fundamental question of how we can become more fully human, bringing something completely new to the development of humanity as a whole. Following the premise of the 'Hundredth Monkey', a few people working to develop and change themselves can make dramatic impacts on the development of all of humanity and human con-sciousness.

Meditation, simply put, is a process of creating calm and focus. The practitioner consciously creates a space in his or her day that is dedicated to practising self-development exercises. These can be as varied as studying a natural object, speaking or contemplating a mantric verse, creating a space of deep inner silence and stillness or of contemplating an aspect of one's own being. For some people it seems easy and natural while for others it feels just about impossible. But like any new discipline, it takes practice, daily practice. (A few minutes a day of focused attention is more effective than longer but less regular efforts.) A healthy meditative life should make one more fit to live fully in the world and contribute to the betterment of other people. If pursued only for selfish gains, meditation will lead to scant progress for the individual student or for our world. This is ultimately a path of service and of ever-growing responsibility for all of creation. In the words of John F. Kennedy:

> Ask not what your country can do for you—ask what you can do for your country. Ask not what America will do for you, but what together we can do for the freedom of man.

Taking steps towards knowing and developing yourself, making your way towards freedom and love, creates new possibilities for all. While this is an individual path, ultimately it touches us all.

As stated, there are countless ways to meditate. Some can be very tempting for young people to explore, possibly even before they are ready to handle the consequences of what meditation can kindle in their souls. This final anecdote comes from a teacher who resorted to a path of meditation before she felt grounded and secure enough in her daily life.

What she experienced led her to give up meditation for many years. I offer this account because meditation is a valuable practice for many people. It can be even more beneficial, however, with the grounding and harmonizing influence of the basic, preparatory exercises described in this book. They will pave the way for and can be an essential part of a fruitful meditative practice.

Ten years ago, before I had done much preparation or training, I decided to try meditating. I was using a specific symbolic image like a mantra, when quite suddenly I perceived something from beyond my usual senses. It was not physical but felt very real and unfriendly. I was terrified. I stopped immediately for I knew that I was not ready to discern the difference between fantasy and spiritual reality. I was not safe.

Some years later I discovered and then began practising these basic exercises. I focused on them exclusively for two years, strengthening and gaining confidence in my soul capabilities before returning to meditation. Now I only meditate on any given day if I have done my basic exercises first. I find it helpful to do them with my eyes open so that I can learn to objectively balance physical and spiritual reality.

For people who might be sensitive or more open to subtle impressions, these thinking, feeling and will preparations are essential to give them strength and confidence. With this certainty students will be better able to control and ground their experiences. They will stay more focused and in control.

Teacher
Olympia, Washington, USA

And here are a few final words from Ralph Waldo Emerson:

Finish each day and be done with it. You have done what you could. Some blunders and absurdities have crept in; forget them as soon as you can. Tomorrow is a new day. You shall begin it serenely and with too high a spirit to be encumbered with your old nonsense.

Suggested Further Reading

Below is a list of books containing more detailed descriptions of paths for cultivating soul capacities. There are countless other titles that have informed this book, but the ones below I have found most helpful along my journey.

Omraam Mikhael Aivanhov: *You Are Gods*, Prosveta, 2002

His Holiness the Dalai Lama and Howard Cutler, MD: *The Art of Happiness: A Handbook for Living*, Hodder and Stoughton 1998

His Holiness the Dalai Lama: *How to Practice, The Way to a Meaningful Life*, Pocket Books 2002

Ralph Waldo Emerson: *Nature: Addresses and Lectures*, 1849

Mohandas Gandhi: *Autobiography, The Story of My Experiments With Truth*, Dover, 1983

Byron Katie: *I Need your Love—Is That True?* Rider Random House 2005

Florin Lowndes: *Enlivening the Chakra of the Heart*, Sophia Books 1998

Paramhansa Yogananda: *Autobiography of a Yogi*, The Philosophical Library Inc. 1946

F. Scott Peck: *The Road Less Travelled*, Touchstone 2003

George G. Ritchie: *Return From Tomorrow*, Spire Books 2003

Marshal B. Rosenberg: *Nonviolent Communication*, PuddleDancer Press 1999

Rudolf Steiner: *Autobiography*, Anthroposophic Press 1999

Rudolf Steiner: *How to Know Higher Worlds*, Anthroposophic Press 1994

Rudolf Steiner: *An Outline of Esoteric Science*, Anthroposophic Press

1997. Also available as *Occult Science, An Outline*, Rudolf Steiner Press 1979

Rudolf Steiner: *Guidance in Esoteric Training*, Rudolf Steiner Press 1994

Shunryu Suzuki: *Zen Mind, Beginners' Mind*, Weatherhill 1973